Ohio
BUCKEYE CANDY

Ohio
BUCKEYE CANDY

· *A Sweet History* ·

RENEE CASTEEL COOK

AMERICAN PALATE

Published by American Palate
A Division of The History Press
Charleston, SC
www.historypress.com

Front cover, clockwise from top left: The gold standard from sprinkles to serving platter, a buckeye tray from Tana's Tasty Treats. *Tana's Tasty Treats*; The Buckeye Lady's fan favorite red velvet Stuffed Buckeye™ offering is beautiful inside and out. *Devon Morgan*; A perfect dip, well practiced over the years at Marsha's Homemade Buckeyes. *Marsha's Homemade Buckeyes*; Bellbrook Chocolate Shoppe prefers to leave the toothpick hole as a telltale sign of its buckeye's hand-dipped process. *Bellbrook Chocolate Shoppe.*
Back cover, top: Lohcally's modern take on the classic combination, a bespoke buckeye candy complete with artistic flair. *Lohcally Artisan Chocolates*; *bottom*: It's always a celebration with an official The Ohio State University Buckeye cake from the Original Goodie Shop. *The Original Goodie Shop.*

First published 2023

Manufactured in the United States

ISBN 9781467154390

Library of Congress Control Number: 2023934833

Notice: The information in this book is true and complete to the best of our knowledge. It is offered without guarantee on the part of the author or The History Press. The author and The History Press disclaim all liability in connection with the use of this book.

There is nothing useless in nature; not even uselessness itself.

—*Michel de Montaigne*

CONTENTS

ACKNOWLEDGEMENTS

I've always had a fondness for the classic combination of chocolate and peanut butter, most prominent in my youth through that ubiquitous "cup" in the bright orange packaging (at the time available only in its simplest form, before today's iterations of "big" versions packed with potato chips, pretzels or the other variation of the candy by the same name). It's my favorite type of ice cream (equal opportunity to makers opting for a chocolate base with peanut butter ribbons and those who prefer a peanut butter base with chocolate flecks), my preference for pie and even my toppings of choice for a humble bowl of oatmeal, a basic made better.

But it wasn't until I met my mother-in-law, Jane Cook, native of Cincinnati and longtime resident of Columbus, Ohio, that I met the buckeye. As I grew up just two states away, this circular format—unlike a truffle because the chocolate doesn't fully enrobe the filling—was foreign to me until my twenties. But I caught up quickly, learning from her high standards both for ingredients and stylistic presentation choices (filling the toothpick hole). For many years, Jane led the annual effort at St. Andrew Catholic Church in Upper Arlington, Ohio, where volunteers donate ingredients for weeks leading up to a multi-day, mini-factory, all-hands effort to roll, shape and dip an average of six thousand buckeyes for the holiday bazaar fundraiser. A massive undertaking, the final product is packaged on trays by the dozen, and all are sold out within the first few hours. (They even offer a pre-order option to ensure you don't miss the boat. The largest pre-order on record? Twenty-five dozen.)

So this one's for you, Mrs. Cook, because even if your talents are now mostly dedicated to the Christmas cookie trays lovingly delivered to close family, friends and neighbors by my three elves each Christmas Eve, your buckeyes are simply the most perfect anyone's ever seen, or tasted, and still the standard by which all others are measured, at least in my book.

INTRODUCTION

By definition, the buckeye is a useless (actually poisonous) nut. But the product of Ohio's state tree has become an inspired icon, both as the moniker and mascot of The Ohio State University as well as the inspiration for a treat quite the opposite of its inedible namesake, with nearly six million pounds consumed annually. While considered a classic candy, found throughout the state and shipped to homesick Ohioans throughout the country, the legacy of this confection is fairly recent, dating back to the mid-1960s.

A Timeline of the Term "Buckeye"

Ohioans gained their nickname long before the candy came along, with multiple legends spanning back to the late eighteenth century:

In 1788, Colonel Ebenezer Sproat opened the first court in the Northwest Territory in Marietta and, because of his large stature, was given the name Hetuck by Native Americans, translating to "the eye of the buck" (a male deer). People began calling Sproat "Big Buckeye," and by the 1830s, writers had adopted the term "Buckeye" more widely to refer to the local settlers.

During the 1840 presidential campaign of Ohio native General William Henry Harrison, his opponents used the term in a derogatory manner, as an alternative for "hick." Their efforts included an illustration of Harrison sitting in front of a log cabin in a rocking chair. Turning this into a positive, Harrison rolled out his "Log Cabin Campaign," having amber bottles made in the shape of a log cabin and filling them with whiskey to give to supporters. He also passed out buckeye nuts, and his campaign adopted a logo of a log cabin made from buckeye timbers and decorated with strings of buckeyes. Supporters crafted buttons, necklaces and even canes out of buckeye tree wood.

Harrison's successful election bid solidified the moniker in his campaign song, with lyrics that included:

Oh, where, tell me where, was your Buckeye Cabin made?
Oh, where, tell me where, was your Buckeye Cabin made?
'Twas built among the merry boys who plied the plow and spade,
Where the Log Cabin stood in the bonnie Buckeye shade.
CHORUS: 'Twas built, etc.
Oh, what, tell me what, was that Buckeye Cabin's fate?
Oh, what, tell me what, was that Buckeye Cabin's fate?
We wheeled it to the Capital, and place it there elate,
As a token and a sign of the bonnie Buckeye State.
CHORUS: We wheeled it, etc.
Oh, why, tell me why, did your Buckeye Cabin go?
Oh, why tell me why, did your Buckeye Cabin go?
It went against the spoilsmen—for well its builders knew,
It was Harrison that fought for the Cabins long and true.

Over one hundred years later, the Ohio General Assembly declared the buckeye tree the official state tree in 1953. Around the same time, The Ohio State University officially adopted the nickname "Buckeyes," though their mascot, Brutus Buckeye, would not be introduced for fifteen more years, in October 1965.

A CLASSIC COMBINATION
TURNED CULINARY CONFECTION

Just as Brutus came onto the scene at Ohio State, a local journalist, Gail Tabor, who had relocated to Columbus and married Steve Lucas, a PhD

A Bit More on Brutus Buckeye

Celebrating his fifty-fifth "birthday" in 2020, the mascot was created by students Ray Bourhis and Sally (Huber) Lanyon and introduced at Ohio Stadium at the school's homecoming football game against Minnesota. Long-standing student service organization Ohio Stater's, Inc., which funded both the original papier-mâché version as well as the subsequent, and more weather-friendly, fiberglass version (which featured two faces—a smile when the game was going well and a frown when it wasn't), also held a contest to name the mascot, ultimately selecting Brutus Buckeye, a submission from OSU student Kerry Reed.

In 1967, another student organization, Block "O," took over management of the mascot as part of their role in promoting school spirit until 1974, when control was transferred to Ohio State's cheerleading team, a decision influenced by the athletics department's desire to send Brutus to support the school's Rose Bowl appearance. Minor updates to Brutus's appearance throughout the '80s and '90s were made, "beefing up" his upper body and adding a baseball cap as well as now signature scarlet-and-gray-striped shirt sporting the number "00." In 2007, the mascot was inducted into the Mascot Hall of Fame and was the Universal Cheerleaders Association mascot national champion in both 2015 and 2019.

While the cheerleading team initially selected Brutus from among its members, separate tryouts were opened up in the spring of 1981. Since then, students wishing to represent the school as Brutus Buckeye and meeting eligibility requirements (regarding student status and minimum grade point average) are able to showcase skills related to personality, creativity and crowd interaction in hopes of being selected. It is viewed as a true honor and privilege to continue the mascot's long-standing legacy. Typically, six to eight students are selected annually for the role, sharing responsibilities for activities ranging from sporting events to community outreach, commercial shoots and even weddings/private celebrations.

FIVE FUN FACTS:
THE BUCKEYE TREE AND ITS FRUIT (SEED)

1. Native Americans used buckeyes—slightly poisonous but not totally useless—for leather tanning, as a salve for rashes and cuts and even as a protein source after boiling and leaching the toxins.
2. Pioneer families also made use of the tree and its fruit, making soap from the kernel of the buckeye seed, carving children's cradles from the tree's wood and even making artificial limbs before synthetic materials were created.
3. The largest buckeye tree in Ohio (in the town of Greenwich, Huron County) was unseated, as a taller version of the species was found in Illinois in 2008 (Oakbrook on the site of the former McDonald's campus).
4. Buckeyes have traditionally been considered good luck, and lore even extends to their role in curing ailments such as rheumatism.
5. Seven species of buckeye trees are native to the United States, with all but the California buckeye found in the eastern half of the country. The Ohio buckeye (*Aesculus glabra*) is prized for its flowers in the spring and striking shades of orange and yellow in the fall. Buckeyes themselves can be harvested from early September to late October, when their husks fall from the tree and are able to be opened.

student at Ohio State, received a Christmas candy from her mother, Sadie. After asking for the recipe for the chocolate peanut butter ball, Gail re-created them, but before fully enrobing the small ball of filling, she lifted up the toothpick and said to her football fanatic husband, "Hey, it looks like a buckeye." The name stuck as Gail began making them for friends and family, all of whom begged her to share her recipe. She initially refused, keeping it a secret until she and Steve left Ohio in 1971. At the same time, a couple they were friendly with also left for Oklahoma. The wife of Steve's classmate swore she would never share Gail's recipe but broke that promise in 1973, submitting the recipe under her own name to the

GO BIG AND GO BUCKEYES

- One of Columbus's oldest candy companies, Anthony-Thomas sells a 235-pound buckeye (made using a copper kettle as a mold), always on display in the lobby of its headquarters shop, for the nominal fee of $3,500.

Anthony-Thomas's factory store location features a larger-than-life buckeye. *Nick Trifelos.*

- The award for the largest buckeye candy made to date goes to Marsha's Buckeyes of Perrysburg, which in 2018 created a record-setting 338.8-pound treat for the Ohio State Fair. With 75 pounds of peanut butter, 75 pounds of margarine, 10 pounds of chocolate and a whopping 150 pounds of powdered sugar, the giant confection measured four feet wide and four feet tall.

- The buckeye was ranked #15 among America's favorite signature Christmas foods in a 2021 survey, besting pecan pie, cranberry sauce and candy canes.

- Spotted by Columbus Food Adventures (@cbusadventures) at the July 2022 Ohio State Fair, one vendor's offering of deep-fried buckeyes took the treat to the next level, becoming ultimate fair food—wrapped in bacon and dusted with powdered sugar.

- The Buck-Guy was created in 2008 by Lori McClung, owner of One Sweet Buckeye, to resemble Brutus, the OSU Buckeyes' mascot. Her homemade confections can be special-ordered via social media (@onesweetbuckeye) or found at various Columbus-area markets, including Kuhlwein's Farm, the Hills and the Morgan House.

The Buck-Guy, an edible homage to The Ohio State University mascot, Brutus Buckeye. *One Sweet Buckeye.*

Ohio State alumni magazine. It wasn't until 1983 that, at the urging of a friend, Gail was convinced to set the record straight, publishing her story and recipe claiming her rightful ownership of the original buckeye recipe.

THE ORIGINAL BUCKEYE CANDY RECIPE

Buckeye Balls

As shared by Gail Tabor in the Arizona Republic, *December 28, 1983.*

4 pounds powdered sugar
1 pound butter
6 or more tablespoons peanut butter
2 teaspoons vanilla
12 ounces chocolate chips
1 block canning wax

Combine first four ingredients, adding a bit of milk if necessary. Roll into small balls. Melt chocolate chips and canning wax in top of double boiler. Make sure chocolate and wax are mixed well so wax doesn't rise to the top. With toothpick, dip the balls into the chocolate, but do not cover completely. Chill in refrigerator. After chocolate is hardened, store candy in plastic bags in freezer.

From holidays to tailgates, it's not a party in the Buckeye State without a tray of tempting treats. (As the saying goes, good luck eating just one.) And while many Ohio families still follow in the footsteps of the Tabor/ Lucas clan making their own homemade versions of this perfectly simple (and sinfully perfect) treat, it didn't take terribly long for chocolate makers throughout the state to jump on board.

IT'S MADE OF PEANUT BUTTER AND CHOCOLATE... BUT DON'T DARE CALL IT A REESE'S

Decades before Gail Lucas coined her buckeye confection, a struggling dairyman named Harry Reese first combined peanut butter and chocolate in cup form, giving the world its #2 best-selling candy (behind only M&Ms), the Reese's Peanut Butter Cup. Reese worked on a farm owned by Milton Hershey, of Hershey's chocolate fame, and first developed the confection in 1928, later selling his H.B. Reese Candy Co. to Hershey for $23.5 million in 1963—just around the time Ms. Lucas was putting her spin on the classic flavor pairing to make it Ohio's own.

CHAPTER 1

THE LEGENDS OF
THE BUCKEYE'S LEGACY

Ms. Lucas's legacy spread fast and far as confectioners across the state adopted the new treat in earnest, building buckeye businesses, even one based on nothing but. Spiraling out from the center of the state and its capital of Columbus, the candy became a cornerstone of chocolatiers north to south, from the other "Big Cs"—Cleveland and Cincinnati—to mini metropolises such as Dayton and Akron-Canton and small-town mom-and-pop shops (some of which have grown into multi-location empires) all along the way.

When it comes to what makes a legend in the legacy of the buckeye candy, emphasis ranges from sheer production volume to association with the institution whose mascot shares its name and includes purveyors dedicated to maintaining handcrafted quality alongside those committed to a greener future for chocolate (in terms of the environment, not the product color). While some were early adopters of the confectionary craze, having perfected their version of the buckeye for generations, others initially sat on the sidelines, debating for decades whether the creation was better suited to home cooks. But ultimately, each of the following shops came to produce a high-quality product that their loyal fan base believes is the best in the business, the ultimate interpretation and the highest homage to their hometown.

ANTHONY-THOMAS CANDY COMPANY

Nick Trifelos proudly carries the fifth generation of his family's business into its seventh decade, but their origins in candy making go back even further—an extra forty-five years, in fact. For it was in 1907 when Trifelos's great-great-grandfather Anthony Zanetos immigrated to the United States from Greece at the age of eighteen, finding his way to Columbus, Ohio, and getting his start as an apprentice in a local candy shop.

Anthony chose Columbus because it was, at the time, one of the pockets throughout the United States where large Greek communities had settled. In Columbus, they founded the Greek Orthodox church on High Street near downtown. Much as it is today, the city then was a great place to start a business, especially a food-based one, because of its true melting pot of cultures and "ability to serve as a micro representation of the country at large, representing a similar demographic of the total states," says Nick, adding, "Restaurants and food businesses see if they can succeed here."

Anthony learned quickly and, in 1916, went into business for himself, forging a path that would shape the next four generations of his family, starting with his son, Tom. Having opened the Co-op Dairy on the corner of Chicago Avenue and Broad Street in Franklinton in 1932, Anthony dreamed of eventually making it a father-and-son operation. Upon Tom's return from service in World War II in 1945, the pair replaced the dairy with Anthony's Confectionary, leveraging Tom's veteran status to obtain a thirty-thousand-pound-per-year allotment of sugar in a time when sugar was rationed.

The pair's partnership grew when, in 1947, they opened the Crystal Fountain Restaurant, also on Broad Street, expanding operations to include ice cream making, a soda fountain and a lunch counter. Customers coming in for one of these other motivations in turn bought more candy, until the candy business became the lead sales generator of the operation. Capitalizing on the demand for their quality confections, Tom and his father decided to focus on it full time, rebranding the company using their first names and becoming the Anthony-Thomas Candy Company in 1952. A child at the time, now company president, third-generation Joseph Zanetos saw the company grow, expanding in 1969 to a sixty-thousand-square-foot facility to continue supporting their retail stores as well as developing wholesale and private label operations. His daughter Candi Zanetos Trifelos, now vice president, also began working at the company at a young age, first in high school and then taking over the retail division upon graduation from college, making a large impact on marketing and merchandising.

In 1995, operations outgrew the Broad Street facility, which caused the company to move to its current home, a 152,000-square-foot factory on the near west side of Columbus. Today, an average of fifty thousand pounds of candy is made over two shifts daily to support the company's thirteen local retail outlets (all within a twenty-five-minute drive), as well as both its fundraising and contract manufacturing divisions. In a tradition started by Joe at the previous facility, the new factory is also open to public tours (booked online), with a glassed-in third-floor catwalk giving a bird's-eye view of the machinery. Nearly thirty thousand people visit each year, including an open house around the Easter holiday that has welcomed up to six thousand people with free samples.

Joining the organization in the spring of 2020, Nick's role as national sales manager brings the fifth generation into the fold to continue the growth trajectory of one of the largest family-owned and operated candy companies in the Midwest. "The candy industry is largely family owned because it tends to be a family business," he says, noting that "most don't make it past the third generation before they sell or fade out." His family

WORLD'S BEST CHOCOLATE MOLDS

Always the entrepreneur, in 1994, Joe Zanetos developed a side business built solely to improve the quality of the molds used for solid chocolate shapes, especially seasonal bestsellers such as Easter's quintessential chocolate bunny and Santa for the holidays. While previously made of metal such as steel or copper coated with tin or nickel, these molds used clamps to hold them together and often required significant cleanup and smoothing after unmolding. Joe's invention leveraged plastic molds with magnetic closures and finger grips for easy, cleaner removal, as well as a "chocolate braille" system that allows filling machines to read exactly how much chocolate is needed for a particular shape. Though the business was sold in 2014 to Tomric (tomric.com), a leading single-source solution for chocolatiers in North America, the molds still bear a signature touch included by Joe: a small butterfly integrated somewhere in each design. When he travels, even overseas, Joe often checks the chocolates to see if he's had a hand in the process.

Left: A selection of Anthony-Thomas specialties. *Anthony-Thomas Candy Co.*

Below: Nick Trifelos, national sales manager and fifth generation of the family behind the Anthony-Thomas Candy Company, appears on QVC to share the company's buckeye candy, which sold out quickly during the segment. *Anthony-Thomas Candy Co.*

Opposite: It's a sweet life for the members of the Zanetos-Trifelos families, multigenerational stewards of the Anthony-Thomas Candy Company. *Anthony Thomas Candy Co.*

maintains relationships with others throughout the state, such as Esther-Price, Malley's and Goumas, learning from one another and even traveling together to tour other manufacturers through their involvement in the RCI (Retail Confectioners International). The community and even familial feel is also extended to Anthony-Thomas's roughly two hundred employees, some of whom have been with the organization through half of its life and many of whom have multigenerational connections to the company.

While Anthony-Thomas's history of candy making includes original recipes dating back to 1907, they actually didn't get in on the buckeye craze until 2000. Some in the organization originally hesitated to add it to the lineup, thinking that people wouldn't buy what they were already making at home. "We like to say we didn't invent it [the buckeye], but we perfected it," says Nick, noting that at home, most people use a compound chocolate product (such as chocolate chips), but Anthony-Thomas uses 100 percent real milk chocolate, as well as double-roasted peanut butter for a smoother center. Another signature distinction is that the top layer is actually white chocolate, colored to match the peanut butter, which helps with stability. And the candy has a shiny finish, rather than the matte of most other Anthony-Thomas confections. But rather than use wax, the company's engineers built machines unique to their facility that achieve the desired sheen. The bespoke stage plant machines, designed by veteran plant engineer Paul Reeder, can produce up to 147,000 buckeyes per eight-hour shift. They are then packed by hand into boxes of 6, 12 or 24 or foil wrapped as individual units for inclusion in gift baskets and party trays.

A FEW FAVORITE FAMILY MEMORIES

They start them young in the Zanetos-Trifelos family, and most family members have been called on even in childhood to contribute. Nick and his mom, Candi, recall their fondest childhood memories getting their start in the family business:

Nick: "Packing boxes right off the line as a little kid. Grandpa would come in and make seafoam [also known as sponge candy], and my dad and I would go all the way up Ohio selling until it sold out."

Candi: "At around eight years old, working at the Ohio State Fair, the other employee working didn't show up, so I worked the booth myself, using my still-developing math skills to make change."

The item has become the company's largest seller and has been featured across outlets from *Good Morning America* to Fox Sports, even selling out QVC during a holiday special feature. Not only can it be found at the company's stores and website, but it has a large Amazon presence as well as over 130 locations of Rural King and mom-and-pop shops throughout the state. Also driving that success is a partnership with The Ohio State University, of which Anthony-Thomas is the official buckeye candy maker, featuring branded packaging with the school's logo and mascot. As Nick focuses on growing national recognition for Anthony-Thomas branded products, he's off to a strong start, nearly doubling the buckeye business, from twelve million pieces in 2021 to almost twenty-four million in 2022.

In addition to buckeyes, other signature items include the buttery English toffee, a fan favorite, and Nick's personal go-to, the dark cherry cordial (ranked #1 AmazonChoice), which offers the novelty of being foil wrapped, creating a little ritual moment for the sweet cherry mixed with dark chocolate and fondant. Both have been featured in partnerships with other community-owned businesses, including longtime restaurant legend Schmidt's Sausage House and newer-to-the-scene Wizard of Za. Even the well-respected Columbus craft beer scene has gotten in on the goods, with the U.S. headquarters of the Scottish BrewDog introducing Anthony Thomas Porter, on tap in the fall of 2022. Described by the brewer as a robust porter base with "50 pounds of Anthony-Thomas Chocolate [added] to the whirlpool," it's said to have "notes of nuts, coffee and of course, rich chocolate."

Nick has his sights on continued growth, including more retail stores and a potential factory expansion. He shares the passion and love for the candy-making business with the generations before him, saying that rather than building the business to sell in hopes of retirement, the family mentality is that "we don't believe in retirement; we want to be here." And those in Columbus, throughout Ohio and even beyond are happy to hear it, knowing that those top-selling buckeyes will stay safely in the hands of those who perfected them.

WITTICH'S CANDY SHOP

Circleville, Ohio, stakes a claim no other town can—it's home to the nation's oldest family-owned and operated candy shop. Celebrating 182 years in business in 2022, Wittich's is equal parts local legend and community institution, led currently by the fourth generation of the Wittich family. But it was a mere accident that the family's legacy became chocolate making instead of book binding and that their ancestors' emigration landed them in Circleville instead of Cincinnati.

Wittich's buckeyes, piled high. *Wittich's Candy Shop.*

Gottlieb F. Wittich, known as G.F., captured his family's arrival in his 1830s journal, named "Reminiscences, Number 3":

> *In the meantime one of the passengers on our boat went up town to purchase some small article and stopped in a Jacob Mader's bakery on Main Street. Mr. Mader inquired of him if any more emigrants were on board of the boat. The young man described the names and occupation of our family and Mader said at once, "These are the people I have been waiting and watching for." Brother F[erdinand] had told Mader that most likely we would pass Circleville on the canal on our way to Cincinnati. He asked him to make inquiry at all the boats going south, in order to stop us from going farther. He came to the boat and informed father that Brother F[erdinand] was located here permanently. In a short time Mader brought him down and all of us were glad to meet him and have our journey ended.*

But G.F. and his brother found that there wasn't enough work for their skill of book binding, and so in May 1837, they made their way on to Cincinnati, where the journal resumes:

> *We were kindly received by Mr. Joseph P. Mayer and his aged parents, who resided with him in the store—and manufacturing—building. I engaged myself to two years at the salary of $4.00 per month for the first year and $6.00 the second….John Myers a somewhat experienced apprentice and myself did most of the work in the manufacturing department under the tuition and supervision of Mr. Mayer, making stick candy, platted, crimped and bar candy, gumpaste work, panwork, rock candy, baking a variety of cakes and pies, ornamenting cakes, compounding cordials and making ice cream.*

This experience paid off when G.F. was summoned back to Circleville by his mother in 1839 after the death of his father. Though he'd hoped to continue honing his new craft at other establishments, G.F. instead used them to open his own shop in 1840, beginning a legacy that future generations of the Wittich family would carry forward. Current owner Janet Wittich, wife of fourth-generation proprietor Fred Wittich, who ran the business together up until Fred's passing in 2015, recalls learning the ropes from her mother-in-law, Frances. During Janet's first holiday season working at the store, Frances pulled her aside to ask if a loyal customer, a local physician, had come in for his usual order yet. Confused, Janet told Frances that no, he hadn't been in, nor had he placed an order. Frances suggested she set aside seven pounds of vanilla buttercreams, certain he would pick them up. Janet did, and thankfully so, as when Christmas drew closer, he arrived to buy just that.

Janet remembers other customers by their orders as well, including a gentleman who visits the store prior to any trips he takes to buy Wittich's peanuts, saying that the people he visits have come to expect them. Fred, too, knew many of Wittich's longtime patrons, saying in a 2010 interview that when the shop was in a previous location at 221 East Main Street, he "would have customers come in that were very well on into their senior years. But they remembered coming to the candy shop and I would hear many of them say, 'The highlight of the week was coming to Circleville on Saturday and doing our shopping because at the end of the shopping spree they would stop at Wittich's Candy to get a hot fudge sundae.'"

At another previous location, 105 West Main Street, Wittich's shops included a soda fountain, a piece of nostalgia Fred long desired to bring back to the current shop at 117 West High Street. So, in 1997, upon the closing of Beechwold Pharmacy, the last to have an operational soda fountain in Columbus, Fred purchased their beautifully maintained soda fountain. It was an endeavor to bring the piece down from the Clintonville neighborhood to Circleville, taking Fred and Janet three days to disassemble the fountain, transport it to their shop and have a plumber install each component. Beechwold Pharmacy owners Arden and Pat Englebach, who had been introduced to Wittich's by their neighbor Bob Eagle of Eagle Family Candy, came down to help train employees on how to craft sodas the proper way, even sharing a recipe book original to the fountain. As an homage to the shared legacy, the fountain topper reads "Wittichs Beechwold Fountain."

And it's not just nostalgic vibes at Wittich's but a tradition of using the same recipes as earlier generations. Many things are still done the same way they have been over nearly two centuries, including employees hand rolling cream centers for flavors ranging from classic vanilla, chocolate, orange, mint, maple, pistachio, black walnut and coconut to the seasonal specialty, pumpkin. They tried once to automate the process using a piece of equipment called a cream depositor but after one trial decided that the more time-consuming method of hand rolling would still be easier, so the machine rests in the attic storage room. Only a slight update has been made for the caramels, offered in vanilla, vanilla nut and chocolate, to use a mechanized cutting machine rather than hand slice—but all are still hand dipped in either milk or dark chocolate. Honeycomb and peanut butter chips

Pretty packaging including an indication of what's inside. *Wittich's Candy Shop.*

round out the assortment, but of course, it's the buckeye that's a best-selling customer favorite.

Wittich's buckeyes are distinct, with a white chocolate option in addition to the traditional milk as well as dark. They also differ from other producers in the fact that they are fully coated in chocolate and dotted with a peanut butter coating to maintain freshness. Lucky visitors to the shop, which participates in the Buckeye Candy Trail, might get a chance to see them dipped by hand and can also sample them at the soda fountain as a feature of the Buckeye Blast Sundae: Smith's Buckeye Blast ice cream topped with chocolate and peanut butter sauce, real whipped cream and a Wittich buckeye.

Whether you visit Circleville on a casual day trip from Columbus or come for a scheduled weekend event such as Chocolate Walk or the famous Circleville Pumpkin Show, a four-day festival held each fall, a visit to the vibrant small town can't be complete without a stop at Wittich's Candy Shop. Sign their guest book to join the generations of patrons continuing the over 180-year tradition, of which Fred considered himself less owner and more "curator of a piece of history." Janet and her three children, the fifth generation, plus their dedicated staff, keep this family legacy thriving as a cornerstone of the town that has loved it for nearly two centuries.

CIRCLEVILLE PUMPKIN SHOW: THE "GREATEST FREE SHOW ON EARTH"

Held the third Wednesday through Saturday each October, the Circleville Pumpkin Show brings over 400,000 visitors annually to a town of just 12,000. In addition to competitions for the largest signature squash and its edible counterpart, the pumpkin pie, festival attendees devour approximately 23,000 pumpkin pies and 100,000 pumpkin donuts. For its part, Wittich's makes nearly two thousand pounds of fudge (another slightly "modernized" part of their operation that required the addition of a hydraulic lift for moving large batches of fudge, allowing one person to do the job that used to take two) and eight hundred pounds of peanut brittle to sell at both their festival booth and storefront.

HONADLE'S FINE CHOCOLATES

Once an Akron institution, Honadle's Fine Chocolates disappeared for over twenty years until third-generation owner Bob Hohenadel (spelled phonetically for purposes of the business name) rebirthed his grandfather's passion for candy making from his home kitchen in 2005.

Honadle's original iteration dates back to 1927, when Lester Hohenadel, then a pretzel salesman in the Greater Akron region, was looking to expand his product offering and had customers asking him about chocolate. Friendly with father-and-son candy-making team Gilbert and Harry London, Lester approached them and gained both a business partner, starting a candy company with Harry, as well as a wife, marrying Harry's younger sister Nellie. Learning from the successful family business, which was firmly rooted in Canton, Lester and Nellie found success in the Akron area, producing and selling chocolates from a factory on State Road in Cuyahoga Falls. The pair grew their family alongside their business, with all eight children working in some capacity as the operation grew to fifteen stores in three states. At its peak, Lester and Nellie's Honadle's produced roughly three thousand pounds of candy per day.

Retiring in 1965, Lester passed the business on to his children, including son Paul, who moved from vice president of manufacturing into leadership.

Say it phonetically—and with chocolate—Honadle's. *Honadle's Fine Chocolates.*

The 1970s saw challenges for the now large company, eventually forcing the family to close their doors and sell the buildings, equipment and other business assets to a Detroit-area candy maker. But the family retained its recipes, which Paul's son Bob resurrected as a side gig to his full-time IT analyst career at Goodyear. Paul cautioned Bob about the difficulties of the business but also offered advice as Bob worked to restart former Honadle's accounts throughout Northeast Ohio. He also reconnected Bob with Honadle's previous suppliers to ensure the product would taste the same as customers remembered.

Starting slow, Bob spent the first fifteen years growing the business part time as he worked to perfect signature recipes for homemade marshmallow and creams, including lemon, maple, orange and Madagascar vanilla bean. Scaling down from the once much larger production volume, Bob's brother Rick helped him adjust quantities for smaller batches, while Bob himself made small improvements. With ambition to be the absolute best iteration of each offering, Bob focused on making every single product by hand. And customers noticed the attention to detail, with some even recognizing the new iteration of Honadle's offering by taste before seeing the name. As he reintroduced the brand, Bob came across many people in

Namesake Treats

Bob Hohenadel quite literally dreams of chocolate. The namesake treats he's developed for each member of the family are creations he says he "dreamed up at 3:00 a.m.," inspired by favorite flavor profiles and signature mix-ins of each of his three children, all of which have also become fast favorites of Honadle's fans:

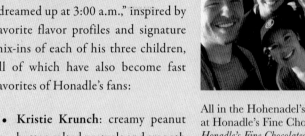

All in the Hohenadel's family at Honadle's Fine Chocolates. *Honadle's Fine Chocolates.*

- **Kristie Krunch**: creamy peanut butter, salted pretzels and smooth buttery caramel enrobed in milk or dark chocolate
- **Brittany Bar**: homemade whipped chocolate blended with large pieces of pecans, cashews and almonds covered in rich milk or dark chocolate and sprinkled with sea salt
- **David Delights**: a take on the campfire classic s'more with whipped chocolate cream and homemade marshmallow layered between graham crackers and double dipped in smooth milk chocolate, topped with a white chocolate drizzle

A few other family members are in on the action as well, including an homage to an offering created by the original store's ownership for Bob's sister Becky, which he brought back, as well as a creation by son-in-law Casey, whose winning combination for the center of his custom Easter egg was such a hit it had to be added to the product line full time:

- **Becky Bars**: creamy peanut butter, roasted and salted cashews and smooth buttery caramel enrobed in rich milk or dark chocolate
- **Casey Crunch**: a delicately flavored whipped mint chocolate and pretzel center covered in smooth milk or dark chocolate and topped with cacao nibs

Next up? Bespoke combinations for each of Bob's three grandsons, which are in the works.

the community for whom his family's chocolates brought back memories, including one who visited Honadle's stores with her grandmother as a child and now ships boxes to her all the way in Japan. Others found boxes and shopping baskets from the original stores and gifted them back to the family.

While the products were initially distributed through retailers who likewise recalled positive affiliation with his father and grandfather's company, by 2019, the company had grown large enough to open a retail store in Hartville, midway between Akron and Canton, and Bob "retired" to focus solely on Honadle's. It was once again a family affair. Bob's wife, Sheryl, as well as three children—Kristen, Brittany and David—all help out in the business, as well as sons-in-law Christopher and Casey. Each has their own specialty, dividing up duties such as packaging (Kristen's talent), while Brittany helps Bob make chocolates. Raised while watching the rebirth of their family's chocolate company, Brittany remarks on seeing firsthand the "immense care, hard work and passion that goes into everything we do at Honadle's and is evident in our chocolates." She adds, "Being able to build relationships with each and every person who walks through the door is our favorite part. Building community through the love of chocolate."

In addition to the Brittany Bar, her namesake treat (Bob has crafted a special item for each family member; see sidebar), Brittany's rotation of go-tos includes items such as peanut clusters, chipotle peanut butter and Xtra dark truffle. Fan favorites include pecan snappers, sea salt caramels and heavenly hash, a signature combination of homemade marshmallow topped with salted pecans. Seasonal features include hand-dipped caramel apples in fall and chocolate-covered strawberries dipped to order for Valentine's Day. And then there are the buckeyes, which Brittany feels are among the best in the area, partiality aside. "We make a bakery-style buckeye." she says, which are hand rolled and hand dipped, adding, "They are made with a perfect blending of Madagascar vanilla, a custom peanut butter blend, and then hand dipped in our creamy milk or dark chocolate."

They're also featured in a newer expansion of Honadle's product line, a house-made recipe of ice cream that Bob spent two years perfecting. The best-selling buckeye flavor features a Madagascar vanilla base with buckeye batter and extra dark chocolate chips mixed in, then topped with a creamy peanut butter sauce and, of course, a Honadle's buckeye. Other flavors include classics like pistachio, cherry vanilla and butter pecan, alongside sea salt caramel, seasonal Key lime and layered Italian spumoni.

Bob Hohenadel's handmade chocolates, a rebirth of his family's legacy. *Honadle's Fine Chocolates.*

ALL IN THE (EXTENDED) FAMILY:
HARRY LONDON AND WAGGONER CHOCOLATES

Lester Hohenadel was in good company when he connected with Gilbert and Harry London, whose work would inspire not only his own business but that of Harry's future son-in-law Cedric T. Waggoner. And while Harry London's chocolates no longer exist, the legacy lives on through both the current iteration of Honadle's and a rebirth of Waggoner by Cedric T.'s son Cedric J., also known as Joe. To see how these stories are interwoven, one must start with Harry, who first started making chocolate confections one hundred years ago.

As the oldest of eight children, Harry Alfred London was responsible for helping to support his family, which meant that during a tough financial time when he was only in fourth grade, Harry quit school and moved from his hometown of Reynoldsville, Pennsylvania, to work at the Republic Steel Corporation in Youngstown, Ohio. In his free time, Harry took up his father Gilbert's tradition of making handcrafted chocolates using European recipes passed down through generations of the London family. These treats were originally given to family and friends at Christmastime, but they began requesting to purchase his treats to share with others, and at his father's urging, Harry quit the steel mill at age twenty-two and began a small chocolate-making operation from the basement of his home in Canton. Applying both his skills as a chocolatier and those of equipment making, Harry mastered the process, and business grew steadily through the decades. Surviving both the loss of his first wife and a fire that destroyed the home he'd built the business from, Harry and his second wife, Iola Campbell, built their first factory at 1281 South Main Street in North Canton in 1954.

Before Harry's passing in 1969, his stepdaughter Bonnie and her husband, Cedric T. Waggoner, joined the family business. The pair expanded both the company's product offering and footprint, adding factory locations and international sales. In the late 1980s and early '90s, their three children, Mercedes, Cedric J. (Joe) and Allison, became the third generation to guide operations forward, in addition to Mercedes's husband, Peter Young. Responsible for modernizing the plant, Joe returned from four-year service in the army in 1987 and began studying emerging global technologies to automate processes without sacrificing key steps to keeping Harry London's handmade quality. Similar to Harry's original prowess in building bespoke equipment, Joe leveraged technologies from outside the confections industry to revolutionize the candy-making process, including the company's best-selling Ohio original, the buckeye.

After eighty years in business, the family faced a difficult decision, ultimately selling Harry London to Alpine Confections in 2003. (The Utah-based company would later acquire legendary Chicago chocolate maker Fannie May, producing both lines out of the Canton factory successfully until it sold both brands to first 1-800-Flowers.com in 2006, which kept the sub brand alive, and subsequently to the U.S. arm of Italian confectionary giant Ferrero in 2017, after which the Harry London brand was slowly retired.) Separately, Joe decided to resurrect the family's original factory, giving it new life as Waggoner Chocolates. Since 2003, he and his team have grown to produce over one hundred varieties of individually wrapped bulk and seasonal offerings, selling across the United States and Canada, as well as Europe and China.

Joe's commitment to carrying on Harry London's legacy comes through, especially in Waggoner's signature buckeye, which Cleveland-area candy shop All City Candy deemed an admirable homage. Waggoner offers both milk and dark chocolate buckeyes, in both regular size and mini, which they deem perfect for "home baking, ice cream and snacking alike." Staying true to its long lineage of candy making, Waggoner says it "believe[s] in tradition and providing our customers with products and packaging that will be remembered, just as Harry London did nearly 10 decades ago."

From the Londons to the Waggoners to the Hohenadels, the Canton area holds a special distinction as the birthplace of not one but three successful candy businesses, carried forward through the decades by multiple generations of each family. Even though Harry's namesake is no longer, his legacy lives on in the timeless tradition he inspired and the happiness it brings to current customers of both Joe's and Bob's thriving businesses.

With an eye toward continued growth, the family focus is on expansion of the business into additional and larger locations, as well as potential bakery and coffee offerings. While they stay true to the classics, they're always open to experimenting with the newest sweet tooth trend, so long as it aligns with their mission of using high-quality ingredients in unique recipes, all handmade in small batches by Bob himself, who coined their slogan, "A Timeless Tradition…Taste the Difference."

WINANS CHOCOLATES + COFFEES

When the local newspaper asked Wilson Reiser's grandfather Max Winans about his high school extracurriculars, the idea of turning his response—a hobby of making chocolates—into a multigenerational family legacy was still just a dream. But since October 1961, when Max and older brother Dick opened Winans Carriage House Candies in their quaint hometown of Piqua, Ohio, it's been a sweet reality for future generations, including Wilson's parents, Max's daughter Laurie and her husband, Joe Reiser. Each generation has brought new life into the family business, including a complementary venture into specialty coffee and expansion beyond that first historic carriage house to now twenty retail locations.

Even before the brothers caught the candy-making bug while making fudge with their babysitter, the family was involved in baking and confectionary businesses starting in the early 1900s. The boys spent time in their grandfather's and father's bakeries, enjoying myriad chocolate products. Upon opening their own shop, they produced hardtack, a vintage candy related to rock candy, and hand-dipped chocolates then referred to as piquettes, clusters of pecans and caramel covered in either smooth milk or dark chocolate. More widely known across the country as "turtles," today Winans calls them Wurtles and offers variations of them with almonds and cashews swapped in for the traditional pecans.

In the 1970s, Max took full ownership of the business and continued running it until June 1993, when Laurie and Joe bought it from him. The couple had taken a trip backpacking in Japan when Joe caused a spat by spending most of one day's budget on a cup of gourmet coffee. Upon returning, he worked tirelessly to duplicate his experience with that "perfect" cup of coffee, knowing it would be a perfect pairing with the family's chocolates. The hard work paid off when Winans added small batch roasted coffee to the menu, making Piqua the first town in Miami County to have specialty coffee and opening the doors of expansion to a second location in Troy, Ohio, under the name Winans Chocolates + Coffees.

Over the past twenty-five years, Winans has bridged the gap between a coffee company and a deeply experienced confectioner, paving the way for bespoke beverage creations such as the Wurtle. The Wurtle is the drink version of the aforementioned Winans take on the turtle candy—a combination of robust espresso with your choice of milk flavored with praline pecan, fine chocolate and caramel. An instant crowd pleaser, this liquid take on the classic chocolate-covered caramel and nut combination comes in your choice of cashew, almond or pecan. Think of it like a caramelly, nutty mocha, served hot or cold.

Back on the candy side of the operation, Winans' year-round favorites include their double dark meltaways, sea salt and wrapped caramels and Miss Clara's pecan toffee. Seasonal specialties include bourbon cherries for the holidays as well as Father's Day and a once-a-year treat of chocolate-covered raspberries especially for Mother's Day. But of course, we're here to talk buckeyes. A top seller and local favorite, Winans has perfected its buckeye over the years, beginning with Max's peanut butter recipe. A decadent, silky formulation, the peanut butter center of Winans' buckeye candy cannot be shaped into spheres by mechanical rolling or depositors. Based on this, for the first six decades, each and every Winans buckeye was hand rolled and hand dipped, with each employee hand rolling at least three trays of buckeyes each morning. Longtime Winans employee and buckeye dipper extraordinaire Bev Synder then individually dipped the delicate peanut butter pieces throughout the day.

An initial effort to mechanize the process involved a modest innovation: a pronged fork-like instrument created by retired Piqua shop teacher Dixon Clement, which allowed for dipping three buckeyes at a time. The tool took top prize as the "Best in Category of New Ideas" when Joe presented it to the Annual Retail Confectioners International Convention.

But it wasn't until Max's oldest grandson, Wilson, left his law career in Columbus to become CEO of the family business in 2021 that further trial and error led him to a new peanut butter molding method, which allows Winans to more efficiently produce buckeyes while maintaining the original recipe. After taking two years to ensure the process didn't affect the product, Wilson remarks, "Our buckeyes are the best in Ohio because of generational stubbornness about quality and acute attention to detail." He notes that the confection is still coddled, as "the peanut butter domes are then hand dipped

The best of both beans—coffee and cacao—at Winans Chocolates + Coffees Roastery. *Winans Chocolates + Coffee.*

in manually tempered chocolate (by a certified Ohio State Buckeye football enthusiast), infusing each confection with an appropriate level of Wolverine-bashing energy." Further, the small hole left from chocolate dipping, which they refer to as the "buckeye belly button," is still hand closed, "because we have never collected buckeyes in The Great State of Ohio with holes in them. Prove us wrong."

Across its product line, Winans also celebrates seasonally, from buckeye apples in fall to peanut butter eggs for Easter. And the classic combination of chocolate plus peanut butter can be found on the other side of the house, with Winans Buckeye Blend Coffee and Buckeye Frapps, available year-round.

While Winans products are sold almost exclusively through Winans stores and online at winanscandies.com, the company ships nationwide as well as to Canada, with Wilson teasing, "Winans buckeyes have been enjoyed all over North America, even in Michigan." One loyal Winans customer sends out six hundred boxes of buckeyes to its business affiliates each holiday season.

Winans prizes this connection to its customers and community, especially its hometown and its support for over one hundred years. Visitors to Piqua can tour the candy kitchen and coffee roastery to see original copper kettles, chocolate enrobers and one of the oldest operating Hobart mixers in the world, which Winans still uses today to make the marshmallow for its Easter eggs. A founding stop on the Ohio Buckeye Trail, Winans was also the shop selected by TourismOhio to provide the incentive for participants of the Buckeye Trail contest in its 2018 inauguration. The winner and three friends were treated to a morning in Winans candy kitchen, making buckeyes with the chocolate experts and taking home a Winans buckeye basket loaded with chocolates and coffees. The company also participates in numerous community events in the towns where it has locations—from the Piqua Taste of the Arts to the Troy Strawberry Festival to ever-popular Chocolate Walks hosted in the Dayton area and other cities around the state.

Wilson credits much of Winans' success to the "special relationship we develop with our customers because of the consistent high quality they can count on," owing that consistency to the "hand-crafted processes to create the chocolate confections" and "the original recipes created and passed down more than sixty years." And he'd know, having begun working for his parents at age twelve and experiencing all aspects, from retail to the chocolate factory, roasting coffee and making deliveries. Passionate about maintaining Winans' handcrafted quality while continuing future expansion, Wilson

CHOCOLATE GOES GREEN

Winans is committed to extending its legacy into the sixth generation and beyond and is making sustainable business choices, including a 2009 move from its carriage house beginnings into the renovated Fort Piqua Plaza, formerly the Fort Piqua Hotel. Subsequently, the downtown location moved again, repurposing the old *Piqua Daily Call* newspaper building to consolidate its chocolate factory, coffee roastery, distribution center and flagship store under one roof. Next in the process is developing a new Winans Roastery out of a building previously used as an automotive repair shop.

Other environmental efforts include:

- Commitment to be net zero carbon across the business by 2040.
- Compostable straws at all locations.
- Biodegradable and recyclable shipping materials.
- Reuse of all cardboard boxes when consistent with sanitary and operations standards.
- Coffee cups are all of the following: Sustainable Forestry Initiative® (SFI®) Chain of Custody Certification (COC), Plant-Based Renewable Resource, Made of 90 Percent Biobased Content and a USDA BioPreferred® Designated Product.

hopes to continue evolving the company both socially and environmentally, as well as providing opportunities for employees and franchisees. "Our goal is to grow to fifty locations by 2030," he says, adding, "We plan to do this by empowering small business owners who want to own their own candy businesses by franchising. Small business is the backbone of our economy today, and we are confident that small business ownership provides a good path to a fulfilled life."

In addition to the long-standing support of its hometown community and those in which it operates, Winans enjoys strong relationships with other family-owned chocolate companies in Ohio and across the country as a member of the Retail Confectioners Association. These connections facilitate a sharing of success stories as well as opportunities for evolution as the industry strives to remain relevant and connect with new generations of consumers. Wilson believes that today that means "more traceable and sustainable ingredients, environmentally friendly packaging, and socially responsible business practices," adding, "Some of these changes may prove difficult to companies that pride themselves on all of the things they have never changed. There are, however, ways that old and new values can be honored simultaneously, and embracing this paradox will be key to the future success of confectioners."

Winans' confidence in its product and pride in its legacy come through as Wilson remarks that rather than compete with other producers, those in the industry help each other in a variety of ways because "there is plenty of love of chocolate to go around and make us all successful."

Marie's Candies

Marie King was a woman of great faith who became faced with great challenge when, in 1941, polio struck her young, hardworking husband, Winfred. The disease left Winfred, originally a farmer, wheelchair bound, and the Kings received help from gracious friends and neighbors, in exchange for which they began gifting them homemade candies. This loving gesture grew steadily into a small business venture, with the couple deciding to open a candy shop in 1956. Three generations later, one of their three sons, his wife and two of their children carry on Marie's legacy well into its sixth decade.

Now known for making over one hundred different types of chocolates, Winfred and Marie's original venture started with an old-fashioned candy, the peppermint chew. The pair purchased a recipe and equipment specific to the pulled mint and molasses–flavored chocolate-coated chewy candy, which had been made famous by Kerr's Candy Kitchen in Urbana, Ohio. The same recipe and candy

The Marie's Candies logo, long a symbol of quality in West Liberty, Ohio. *Marie's Candies.*

A single signature buckeye— simple perfection. *Marie's Candies.*

Remodeled to retain history, the current Marie's Candies location was formerly the town's train depot. *Marie's Candies.*

cutter are still used at Marie's today for the six batches of peppermint chews they produce weekly.

Ten years after opening, the business was successful enough to need more space, so in 1966, Winfred and Marie built a house and candy shop combination at their present location in West Liberty. Quite literally growing up in and with the business, their three sons worked in the candy shop throughout their teenage years, with middle son Jay staying on after Winfred's death, taking ownership of the business in 1977. By 1986, candy operation had taken over the entire building, while Jay and his wife, Kathy, dedicated their lives to improving candy production, increasing their product offering and designing candy-based gifts. They also oversaw the business's next expansion, that of adding and restoring the town's historic train depot to the property as their current retail space. This project took three years, from 1993 to its opening in 1996, just in time to celebrate the shop's fortieth anniversary.

Passing down the reins yet again, Jay and Kathy's son Shannon and daughter Rebecca King Craig became third-generation owners in 2016. Rebecca says the business "continues to thrive because of the use of high-quality ingredients and special customer attention," a signature touch that's never changed. In a tribute to her grandmother, Rebecca helped compile stories and quotes for college volleyball teammate turned English teacher Erin L. Hill to write Marie's book, *Faith, the Only Star: A Family's Journey through Challenge to Victory*. One such sums up the dedication Marie felt for the business, which has carried down from her through the three generations: "Now remember, if you can't work and talk at the same time, you know which one has to go."

That commitment to quality comes through in best-selling products such as butter crunch (toffee), peanut butter fancies (which Rebecca describes as similar to a Reese's Peanut Butter Cup) and Tur'Kins (like a turtle). For her part, Rebecca is partial to Marie's chocolate-covered potato chips, French mints, chocolate-covered Oreos and nut butter crunch. In addition to the

Marie's assortments of milk and dark chocolate delights. *Marie's Candies.*

TRAIN DEPOT TURNED CANDY SHOP

Built in 1926, the West Liberty train depot stood in the southwest corner of the village until second-generation Marie's Candies owner Jay King and his wife, Kathy, purchased the deteriorating building in 1992 with the dream of moving, preserving and renovating it. Keeping a piece of local history in the town was a primary motivation, with some of the lumber dating back to the town's original early 1900s train depot, which had been built by the Big 4 railroad and partially destroyed during a fire. The depot had been taken over by the New York Central Railroad in 1930, servicing both passenger and freight trains during the height of its operations into the early 1940s. Though the last passenger, Bill King (no relation), a World War II serviceman, was given a ticket into the West Liberty Depot on his way home in 1942, freight operations would continue until 1960.

After ceasing functional rail service, the building was used by King Feed and Supply for grain storage until the 1990s. During this period, suggestions were made to either repurpose the building as a library for the town or to move it to the Lions Ball Park, but neither moved forward. Having long considered its potential and meaning to the community, Jay and Kathy became the driving force behind its restoration, having the building pulled across town (roughly three miles) in July 1993. The major undertaking brought out many of the town's residents—and their cameras, with local shop owners recalling all the film in town was sold out that day.

Working with a San Francisco architect, Steve Gray (who has roots in West Liberty), the restoration included an addition for public restrooms, new gutters and paint. A local contractor, Jeff Heiberger, helped rebuild the inside, retaining much of its original design while adapting its use to the needs of a retail space. On Thanksgiving weekend 1996, the new depot opened its doors as Marie's Candies, proudly welcoming people from its new home on the north edge of West Liberty. In retaining some of its historical train depot memorabilia as well as a wall of photos depicting the restorations before and after, Jay and Kathy were able to create a cozy chocolate shop while saving this local landmark.

West Liberty shop, Marie's has one wholesale location, Choffey's Coffee and Confections in Delaware, Ohio, which offers both bulk and prepackaged chocolates, including Marie's buckeyes.

Speaking of those bespoke buckeyes, Marie's are made special with the use of both a secret ingredient and an old piece of candy equipment called a Friend Machine, which forms the smooth peanut butter cream centers into their round shape. The bottom and sides are then twice dipped in milk chocolate. As Rebecca notes, "Not every piece is exactly the same size. The final product is something that looks like a natural buckeye nut and tastes amazing."

Available in quarter-pound sleeves (approximately nine pieces), half- or one-pound boxes (approximately eighteen and thirty-five pieces, respectively), the giftable classic Marie's logo boxes are printed with Ohio and buckeye trivia to test recipients' knowledge. Co-packaged Ohio State University Buckeyes gear ranging from trinket-type keychains and gift card holders to perennial favorite mugs and tumblers to the bit more unusual (but practical!) leaf bags, day packs or Brutus pillow pet cover all of your gifting bases. And Marie's can ship your buckeyes anywhere in the United States, with fall bringing orders from Kentucky to North Carolina, Pennsylvania, Tennessee and, yes, even Michigan. From tailgates (this year, one as far as Florida for OSU v. Notre Dame) to holiday gatherings to wedding season, Marie's buckeyes have also been featured in *Martha Stewart Weddings* magazine twice, in both 2008 and 2012, as the signature Ohio edible favor. Buckeyes are big business year-round.

But if you can make the trip to West Liberty for a stop at Marie's Candies, perhaps while traveling the Ohio Buckeye Candy Trail, on which the shop is a participant, Rebecca says it's "a quaint little village surrounded by farmland." She adds, "There are caverns and castles to explore, as well as snow skiing, gift shops and a restored opera house." And of course, most importantly, "we love to greet our customers with a sample!"

MARSHA'S HOMEMADE BUCKEYES

Marsha Smith fell in love with her mother-in-law's candy as soon as she married her husband, Dave, but none of them could know at the time that the passed-down recipe for a homemade classic would become the basis for a business that has built a following for nearly forty years.

Marsha Smith with her original storage area for a burgeoning buckeye candy business. *Marsha's Homemade Buckeyes.*

Now in its second generation of family leadership with the couple's sons Brad and Matthew leading the future forward as president and vice president, respectively, Marsha's operation has grown in size but remained singular in focus, with one goal: to "produce the perfect peanut butter and chocolate buckeye."

A stay-at-home mom of three, Marsha turned her holiday hobby of candy making into a cottage business back in 1984 after a successful first venture selling her buckeyes at a neighborhood garage sale. Taking over her home kitchen, Marsha recalls many late nights rolling peanut butter balls while the kids slept, slowly taking over the house, first with refrigerators in the living room and, later, a full candy kitchen in the basement. It was a big hit with the neighborhood kids, especially those whose families got recruited to help out during busy times, with adults working on one side of the basement while little ones played on the other. Matt recalls the draw for friends to visit after school throughout both elementary and middle school, as Marsha's operated this way for its first fourteen years.

Marsha Smith hand dipping trays of buckeye candies in her home kitchen. *Marsha's Homemade Buckeyes.*

Securing her first commercial account, local Perrysburg grocer Kazmaier's, gave Marsha the confidence to approach The Andersons in Maumee. As Andersons continued growth, so did Marsha's, adding an account each time they opened a new store. But the business's biggest break came in 1999, when Marsha received a letter from the home office of Cracker Barrel stores, based in Lebanon, Tennessee. She initially thought the communication was a prank being played on her by a local friend until a phone call to the headquarters confirmed that the local Perrysburg store had inquired about carrying her product. She initially agreed to fulfill only the chain's Ohio locations. It was the bump the business needed to find a full manufacturing facility, finally moving out of the Smiths' home. They ramped up production to supply all 650 Cracker Barrel stores, and each location across the United States now carries Marsha's buckeyes. Other national partners now include Kroger, JoAnn and Michael's stores, as well as select Giant Eagle, Meijer, Gordon Food Service, Marc's and, most recently, Dollar General locations. The company is also affiliated with The Ohio State University, a major point of pride for Marsha herself, allowing fans at both the Horseshoe (Ohio Stadium) and Schottenstein Center to enjoy her buckeyes.

As Marsha's has enjoyed incredible growth, the family has focused on retaining its homemade recipe and taste, making only operational changes to production methods such as the addition of a ball rolling machine (this timesaving upgrade alleviates what Marsha felt was the pain point for home producers initially, as while the product itself isn't hard to make, the process is time consuming, too much so for many moms like herself). Its packaging has also become instantly recognizable, with the top-selling deli container, which holds twelve buckeyes, and online fan favorite, the larger-format party tub, which holds fifty, perfect for parties such as gameday tailgates and graduations. Individually wrapped and three-pack options are also popular, as are gift baskets featuring Marsha's buckeyes alongside other Ohio-made products from Taste of Toledo, a gourmet gifting company.

Online sales have boomed in recent years, bringing buckeyes to those outside Ohio, with e-commerce sales manager Zak Kern saying Marsha's product has "crossed EVERY state line, even Alaska and Hawaii," and adding that while the brand ships across the United States but not yet internationally, "customers have traveled overseas with our buckeyes on many occasions and have road tripped across the country as well." Weddings are another popular ordering occasion, with one fan praising Marsha's for shipping trays of buckeyes to New Orleans to supply a bit of Ohio to a Cajun/Creole rehearsal dinner, adding, "The buckeyes disappeared with lightning speed" and were a "true hit, for those who knew what they were and those who had never heard of them."

Marsha's also contributes to charitable events ranging from those of the local high school to the annual Buckeye Cruise for Cancer. And the strong connection with OSU led the company to fulfill a large order in

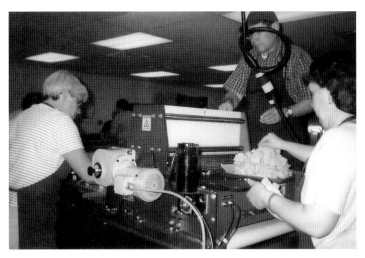

Marsha's expands to machinery, including a peanut butter ball rolling machine and forklift, but the business stays true to its roots, hand dipping and packaging USAToday's 2019 Best Buckeye. *Marsha's Homemade Buckeyes.*

support of the Fisher College of Business's class of 2020's postponed commencement due to COVID-19. An OSU alumnus himself, Brad was happy to participate, helping to provide a sweet spot in a challenging time. Having also felt pandemic pressures due to closures of its restaurant accounts and changes in consumer grocery behavior as well as staffing and freight issues, the opportunity to give back to the university was a win-win for the business.

Back up and running with tours, visitors traveling the Ohio Buckeye Candy Trail can call to schedule a behind-the-scenes look at the work done by Marsha's roughly thirty employees. From mixing of the peanut butter center, to hand dipping the chocolate layer (leaving the toothpick hole unfilled), to hand packing boxes and trays of premium-quality homemade buckeyes, the team can produce up to ninety thousand per day. And their dedication to perfection has paid off, with USA Today's 10Best Reader's Choice poll ranking them the Best Buckeye in Ohio in 2019. This is a strong show for a business built solely on one product and focused for nearly forty years on ensuring it tastes, as one recent customer review put perfectly, "as close to homemade without being homemade!"

ESTHER PRICE

For a young Esther Rose Rohman, it all started in home economics class. A rite of passage for generations (which had all but faded from many schools until a resurgence under the all-encompassing rebrand of family and consumer sciences), it was here where seventh grader Esther learned both the recipe and a love for making fudge, a new skill she excitedly took home to her mother's kitchen, asking if she could make more for family and friends. Just a few years later, faced with the tough choice of whether to finish high school or take a job at Rike's Department Store in downtown Dayton, Esther chose the latter, a fateful decision that would unwittingly springboard her into entrepreneurship.

While working at Rike's, Esther would take in fudge for her coworkers, who instantly fell in love with her handmade delicacy. Loving the praise she received, Esther continued making fudge as often as possible, even after marrying Ralph Price in 1924 and leaving her job to start a family. She'd return to Rike's with her wares, selling fudge to former coworkers to help support her husband and young twins, until a Rike's floorman discovered

Delivering deliciousness to Esther Price's seven retail locations throughout the Dayton and Cincinnati areas. *Kelly Schreck.*

what she was doing and required she sell through the store's candy counter instead. Even though Rike's doubled the price, her loyalists were hooked and happily went down to the candy counter to purchase the pound of fudge Esther had brought for them, immediately establishing Rike's as Esther's first commercial customer.

For the first twenty-five years, Esther produced candy from the kitchen of her two-bedroom house on Fauver Avenue, making candy at night while her children were sleeping. Initially working to expand her business, she would cut, wrap and package the cooled fudge in wax paper, pack it into bags and walk over a mile to the streetcar that would take her downtown, where she would go door to door selling candy to businesses including banks and doctor's offices. Her skills grew alongside her business as Esther started experimenting with dipping her fudge into chocolate and making other small pieces such as candy Easter eggs. From hot plates taking over the kitchen to candy cooling in the basement, a decoration station set up in the attic and customers lining up from her living room out onto her porch to make their purchases, Esther outgrew her home operation, even causing some neighbor complaints to the city due to the cars of Esther's customers causing congestion and traffic.

Stations set up specifically to add Esther Price's signature red ribbon, hand tied and trimmed to perfection by tenured experts. *Kelly Schreck.*

In 1952, Esther purchased two Victorian homes on Wayne Avenue, moving the business there and opening to crowds eager to watch (and sample) candy as it was hand dipped at the same location where the company's entire candy supply is still made today. To maintain quality, Esther frequently worked up to eighteen hours a day, tasting and adjusting each batch by hand, and was able to tell if the chocolate was done just by looking at it. When creating her recipes, she believed that fresh, local dairy products—milk, cream and butter—as well as fine, "fancy-grade" nuts such as almonds, pecans and cashews, made a distinguishing difference in the end product, and she insisted on using only the highest-quality ingredients possible in every piece of candy she produced. Her exacting standards went beyond the product

 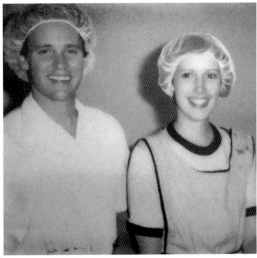

Left: Jim Day with Esther Price, two candy industry legends with a shared legacy. *Right*: Current Esther Price operators Doug and Barb (Day) Dressman. *Esther Price*.

to its packaging, with Esther's gold embossed foil box specifically tipped to have a particular sheen and a signature red ribbon hand tied on every one-, two- and four-pound assortment.

For nearly twenty-five more years, Esther focused on her "uncompromising commitment to customers and quality ingredients," standards that the business continued to uphold under new ownership, which took over in 1976 upon her retirement. Esther sold her business to a group of four friends and Cincinnati-area business owners, Jim Day, Ralph Schmidt, Jim Bates and Joe Haarmeyer. The former two would buy out the latter two just a few years later and operate the business as partners until Schmidt's passing in 2006, after which the Day family took over ownership individually. Committed to carrying forward Esther's formidable legacy, Day was joined by his three daughters and sons-in-law, including youngest daughter Barbara and her husband, Doug Dressman, who now lead the company's operations and provide guidance as members of its board of directors. Day, who operated a concrete foundation company prior to his involvement with Esther Price, was a quick study of the industry, learning from Esther herself and gaining recognition both colloquially, becoming known as the Candyman, as well as professionally, earning induction into the National Confectionery Sales Association's Candy Hall of Fame in 2016. Likewise, Dressman has followed in the footsteps of his father-in-law, recently being nominated for trade association Candy Industry's prestigious Kettle Award.

From copper kettles to "The Beast," to a packaging puzzle, each step of the candy making process is hand-crafted in small batches by Esther Price experts. *Kelly Schreck.*

Helping the Day family maintain Esther Price's original recipes and quality focus, many of the company's employees have been with the operation for more than forty years, spanning departments from production to packaging and lending exacting expertise to each step of the process. Starting their days as early as Esther did, production begins around 4:00 a.m. with caramel and cream centers crafted by longtime cook Stacy Yaney. Once cooled, these concoctions travel to what the team lovingly refers to as "The Beast," a multi-step machine that cuts, coats (top and bottom) and cools each candy as it travels down the line. Each type is "strung" with a specific design, ranging from simple drizzle to hand-drawn heart, indicating its interior contents. After the candies are transferred over to the nearby packaging area, Justina Francis, a forty-five-year veteran, and her team individually select and arrange each assortment, weighing the final package to ensure it meets their minimum (they often err on the side of an overage, giving the customer a bit more than they're paying for, but who doesn't like free chocolate?). While even the company's standard rectangle can be a challenge due to the fact that no two candies are exactly the same size, the heart-shaped offerings popular each Valentine's Day are by far the toughest to pack with their rounded corners and angled point. And last but certainly not least comes that iconic red ribbon, added by a station of experts including Linda Bell, who can hand tie roughly nine hundred boxes in an eight-hour shift, the spools seemingly never-ending, especially during the Christmas holiday season.

Employing over one hundred people per day during its production season, which runs from late August through April annually (the operation shuts down during the off-season to conduct maintenance, repairs and deep cleaning), the relatively modest facility produces 700,000 pounds of candy in just thirty-five weeks, enough to provide year-round supply to its seven retail stores (four in the Dayton area and three in Cincinnati), online webstore and wholesale grocery accounts throughout Ohio, Kentucky and Indiana. Striving for a feeling of sheer joy similar to that of Esther's customers first visiting the Wayne Avenue location, vice president of sales Todd Summers describes a visit to an Esther Price store as "not just a candy store, but a destination," adding that a customer "has to decide to go there, so we want them to have a great experience and leave happy." Growing up in the Dayton area, Todd's favorite since childhood has been the milk chocolate opera cream, a recipe Esther perfected early in her career, which he recalls as the piece he always went for first in the assortment box. "I still ask my mom before I take a piece," he laughs, adding that she visits the

Two takes on the classic combination at Esther Price: milk chocolate and peanut butter buckeyes and peanut butter creams. *Todd Summers and Kelly Schreck.*

shop weekly to buy candy for the women she teaches Sunday school with in town.

In addition to the classic opera cream, longtime favorites among Esther's recipes include all things caramel, especially the shop's take on a turtle, which they call caramel pecans, as well as sea salt caramels and chocolate-covered caramel pretzels. Chocolate-covered cherries (traditional or bourbon) as well as honeycomb chips are also fan favorites, available in either milk or dark chocolate. When it comes to the state's classic combination of peanut butter and chocolate, the brand offers two takes: a signature peanut butter cream made with freshly ground peanut butter hand folded into their buttercream center and, of course, a buckeye, a bestseller especially from the fall football season through the winter holidays. The slightly larger take showcases the company's milk chocolate recipe, highlighting its commitment to quality ingredients. The store has been a stop on the Buckeye Candy Trail since its inception.

Likewise, partnerships with other Dayton-area businesses have created products that allow Esther Price's tradition of excellence to be featured alongside brands such as potato chip maker Mikesells, espresso beans from coffee company Boston Stoker and even a beer from brewer Warped Wing. The latter, called Esther's Li'l Secret, has been an annual collaboration since 2014 and has included variations such as a Chocolate Peanut Brittle Porter, Chocolate-Covered Cherry Stout, Chocolate Sea Salt Caramel Scotch Ale, Double Fudge Cream Stout and Caramel Pecan Scotch Ale. Another Dayton-area institution, Dorothy Lane Market, even tapped the company to create a custom co-branded chocolate assortment in celebration of the grocer's seventy-fifth anniversary in 2023.

Above, left: Dayton brewer Warped Wing puts a sweet spin on its porters, stouts and Scotch ales in a multi-year collaboration with Esther Price. *Todd Summers.*

Above, right: A selection of Esther Price treats including the featured partnership with beloved Dayton potato chip brand Mikesells. *Renee Casteel Cook.*

Left: Two celebrated Dayton stalwarts, Esther Price and Dorothy Lane Market, the latter commemorating its seventy-fifth year in business. *Renee Casteel Cook.*

A FEW MORE OF ESTHER'S LITTLE SECRETS

Three years before her passing, Esther, at age eighty-seven, co-wrote an autobiography with her granddaughter Linda Otto Lipsett. Published in 1991 and titled *Chocolate Covered Cherries: Esther Price's Memories*, the book details her experiences as a young entrepreneur in a time when female-owned businesses were far less common. Recalling everything from struggling to obtain bank loans to leaving the windows of her home open so her neighbor could check on her sleeping twins while she left in the early morning hours to sell door to door, the book is equal parts entertaining memoir and inspirational education.

Looking forward just three years to its own celebration, that of a century in business, Esther Price shows no signs of slowing down and certainly not of compromising on ingredients or tradition. Maintaining its founder's commitment and recipes has kept the company going and growing, a proud stalwart of the Greater Dayton community, of which it shares mutual admiration. After the city experienced a tragic mass shooting in its popular Oregon District in August 2019, the company donated an entire day's worth of sales, totaling $85,000, to the fund supporting victims and their families and subsequently created a Dayton Strong candy bar, from which a portion of proceeds were also donated.

Though Esther herself passed on to that sweet spot in the sky in 1994, one can be certain she'd be proud of the community surrounding and continuing her legacy, of which she was a shining star. Her confections brought joy to many over her ninety years, joy that lives on today and into the future through her recipes and the experience one has when visiting one of her namesake shops. For nine decades, Esther Price has delivered perfectly crafted chocolates from Dayton, Ohio, to loyalists throughout the country and beyond, summing it up by saying, "Quality takes time, and we're ninety-seven years into creating the best chocolate any generation has ever tasted."

TOOTHPICK HOLE OR NO TOOTHPICK HOLE?
THE BURNING BUCKEYE QUESTION (AHEM, DEBATE)

From this book's intro to the stories among its pages, hints have been dropped about an eternal conflict in the world of buckeye producers, be it home cooks or shop owners, as to whether the little hole left behind from using a toothpick (or even two!) to dip the peanut butter ball in chocolate should be subsequently covered up (typically by rubbing a finger over it to close the hole). While owners like Marshall Blose of Bellbrook Chocolate Shoppe insist that leaving the hole is a telltale sign that the product is hand dipped, others take a firm stance on the opposite side, preferring a presentation they deem "prettier."

Taking things a step further, there are those who decorate their buckeyes, be it with festive occasion-based colored sprinkles or even, as in the case of Alicia Hindman, owner and namesake of the Buckeye Lady, ingredients such as M&Ms or red velvet cake that indicate the contents of her stuffed variations, ultimately filling, or at least overshadowing, any divot or dimple.

Truth be told, whether one sides with the purists or the perfectionists on this issue of "taste," ultimately, that itself is thankfully unaffected. So, take the time or skip the step; either way, each equally delicious bite of buckeye is sure to satisfy the sweet tooth. Speaking of debates... do you eat your buckeyes all in one bite or try to take two? An equally contentious matter with every bit as evasive an answer.

The Buckeye Lady's fan favorite red velvet Stuffed Buckeye™ offering is beautiful inside and out. *Devon Morgan.*

CHAPTER 2

A TASTY TRAIL

Since 2018, TourismOhio and the Miami County Visitors Bureau have partnered to showcase producers across the state making Ohio's official candy. Originated by a class of the Ohio Tourism Leadership Academy, an annual program facilitated by the Ohio Travel Association, the idea came from a group project in which one of the group members was an employee of TourismOhio who had been working on the development of tourism trails throughout the state. With topics ranging from food and wine to shopping, history, sights and even coffee, the thought of adding a trail focused on the state's favorite confection was a no-brainer.

Around the same time, Miami County (which includes Dayton and surrounding areas) was nearing the launch of a new website, and TourismOhio approached the organization in partnership to create and house the new trail on their site. The groups collaborated on the inaugural map, which included thirty-one shops throughout the state, selected based on the criteria of being shops that create their own buckeyes versus selling those produced elsewhere. For the launch, each participating business got a window decal indicating their official designation as a trail stop, and a contest was launched for consumers to upload selfies taken in front of/at any of the businesses with their purchases using the hashtags #buckeyecandycontest and #buckeyecandytrail. The winner took home a prize package from participating shop Winans, based in Miami County, including their signature buckeye basket, as well as a trip to Piqua to tour Winans Candy Kitchen and try their hand at making buckeyes with the shop's chocolate experts.

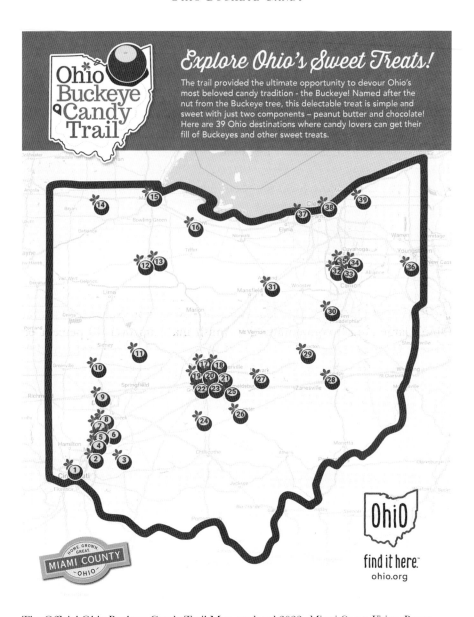

The Official Ohio Buckeye Candy Trail Map, updated 2022. *Miami County Visitors Bureau.*

According to Leiann Stewart, executive director at Miami County Visitors & Convention Bureau, the trail is kept fresh by updating the map annually, with the latest release in May 2022 updated to now feature thirty-nine shops. New producers can submit for inclusion to either/both TourismOhio and the Miami County Visitors Bureau, which continue to work together in vetting new additions (The Buckeye Lady, featured on page 126, has submitted and hopes to be added in the next trail update). To highlight the range of shops on the current trail, next up, we travel the state to take a look at the spin each takes on the classic buckeye, as well as other signature offerings.

COBLENTZ CHOCOLATE COMPANY

Ohio's Amish country is known for many things, from furniture to cheese, but in Walnut Creek, it's all about chocolate. Nestled in Northeast-Central Ohio's large Amish community (the Amish make up over 40 percent of Holmes County's population, one of the largest settlements in the world), Coblentz Chocolate Company has been setting the standard for high-quality handmade confections for over thirty-five years.

Founded in 1987 by husband-and-wife team Jason and Mary Coblentz and Jason's brother Mark Coblentz, the business began with just a few recipes and a love for chocolate. A young couple, then only in their mid-twenties, Jason and Mary were dedicated to the ingredients as well as attention to detail in the chocolate-making process. Making up a few batches in their home kitchen that spring, they taste tested thirty-five different confections, all using very high-quality chocolate, the same that they continue to use today. Fresh, local cream and butter as well as a higher percentage of cocoa butter also give Coblentz recipes a signature taste across best-selling items from caramels to cordials, meltaways to truffles.

Their creations were well received, and on October 30, they opened shop in the charming Victorian home that still houses their retail location, selling over two hundred pounds of chocolate during the first week. The following year, Coblentz would welcome nearly one hundred customers to the store each day for early favorites including peanut clusters and hand-dipped chocolate-covered cherries.

With tourism to the area picking up, word quickly spread of Coblentz's premium product. Mark's connections in the wholesale business allowed distribution to increase to stores throughout Amish country, and a new mail-

Coblentz Chocolate Company, a welcome center for Ohio's Amish country. *Coblentz Chocolate Company.*

Coblentz signature logo chocolates. *Coblentz Chocolate Company.*

order business was created, both of which helped Coblentz to expand their customer base. As Jason and Mary raised their own family of four children, two of whom are still involved in the family business, generations of loyalists introduced first their children and subsequently their grandchildren, growing the Coblentz community and becoming a mainstay for residents and visitors to the heart of Walnut Creek.

Business expansions across Coblentz's product offering, staff and space all continued throughout the '90s. A second kitchen was added in 1991 to meet demand and allow for the introduction of Dutch delights, a line of wrapped chocolates. By 1999, the team of now twenty-four employees was producing two thousand pounds of chocolate each week, consisting of seventy different types of chocolates. The early 2000s saw another expansion, a renovation that added 7,200 square feet to the facility, including new production areas and a viewing gallery for visitors to watch the chocolate-making process. Another signature product offering, Swiss-style chocolate truffles, was added shortly thereafter for the 2002 holiday season.

But 2003 was all about the buckeye. To celebrate the Big Buckeye Birthday Bash in Dennison, Ohio, Jason Coblentz worked directly to make what was at the time the world's largest buckeye candy, weighing in at 275

A Coblentz box of hand-dipped buckeye candies. *Coblentz Chocolate Company.*

pounds. Though an even larger buckeye would eventually be crafted (see page 15), it was quite the way to celebrate Ohio's 200th birthday. Should your appetite not be quite that large, Coblentz offers their assortment of buckeyes in a more typical size (three-pack sampler or fifteen-piece box) as well as in mini form, perfect for snacking. Both sizes consist of a rich, made-from-scratch peanut butter center covered in creamy chocolate—with the minis available in both milk and dark.

Other Coblentz staples include milk and dark sea salt caramels, almond butter crunch, Dutch pretzels and fudge. Coblentz's caramel recipe, used in several of the shop's creations, has been the same since day one—a traditional, time-honored classic—especially when topped off with milk chocolate and roasted salted pecans for the signature pecan snapper. Rounding out the lineup are brittles and barks, caramel corn and the Wunderbar Schokolade, a three-ounce chocolate bar with inclusions ranging from classic almond to trendy sea salt toffee or espresso.

Trendy might seem a strange adjective for a business rooted in nostalgia, but Coblentz strikes the perfect balance of offering products that evolve with consumer tastes while maintaining the experience of a time when visiting the candy shop was an event unto itself. Coblentz keeps an eye on flavoring trends and experiments with inspirations, even introducing cinnamon chili melts, creamy milk chocolate infused with ghost pepper and cinnamon for a "spicy kick."

Since day one, Coblentz has believed in fair trade, which has become increasingly desired by consumers in recent years. Not only has their commitment to quality remained, but the direct connection to the sources of their ingredients has long been a point of pride that is more and more in demand. Surrounded by a hardworking, honest community, Coblentz carries this culture through its practices with its suppliers and farmers. Holding true to the local tradition of doing things the old-fashioned way has helped build a reputation of using only the freshest ingredients and taking no shortcuts, with truffles still hand rolled and chocolates still hand dipped.

There have, however, been a few modernizations to enhance production capabilities and capacity, such as the 2008 additions of a new chocolate melter and cooling conveyor, which opened the way for the introduction of Jason & Mary's Handmade, a line of oversized treats and signature selections. Further expansions in both 2012 (4,500 square feet) and 2016 (10,800) still weren't enough to handle the business's growth, so in 2018, a new production facility was built a few miles from the store. While most

A Coblentz assortment of Amish country chocolates. *Coblentz Chocolate Company.*

of the chocolate making moved to that candy kitchen in 2019, chocolate molding is still done at the retail location, allowing consumers to see this part of the process up close. And for those who want to get even closer to the action, Coblentz hosts an annual tasting event where guests can taste over fifty varieties of chocolate and participate in multiple candy-making activities, taking home what they make.

Another annual event, the Coblentz Christmas Open House, coincides with the Walnut Creek Annual Christmas Tree Lighting, bringing visitors to the charming small town decked out in its holiday finest. Product samples, sales and door prizes draw crowds of adults, while the gingerbread playhouse charms children. Seasonal items include snowmen-shaped chocolate bars, peppermint bark ornaments and chocolate-covered "Santa's Belly" decorated Oreos.

Whether visiting for a classic Christmas or on a sweet summer day, you'll find Walnut Creek full of quintessential small-town hospitality. Scenic views combine with tempting treats for a perfect trip back in time to Ohio's beautiful Amish country and Coblentz's classic confections.

SWEETIE'S CHOCOLATES AT GRANDPA'S CHEESEBARN

It's a tale of two grandpas for the family behind Sweetie's Chocolates at Grandpa's Cheesebarn, a roadside beacon for travelers off I-71 toward Cleveland. First came Grandpa Yarman, who in the early 1900s sold his last possession to purchase a wheel of Ohio Swiss cheese and opened a cheese shop in West Salem that thrived into the 1930s as he expanded operations to smoked meats such as country ham and bacon. Yarman's daughter Vera watched her father's passion for quality, local products, and after she married Dick Baum, the pair continued the family's legacy of selling quality foods sourced locally from throughout the state at Baum's Wonderland of Food, also in West Salem.

Following in the footsteps of Yarman, the Baums sought out the best cheese makers in Ohio, exploring new areas to find best-in-class versions of Swiss and Colby, distinct local varieties, in addition to new meat-smoking techniques. Then in 1978, with daughter Ronda and son-in-law Richard Poorbaugh, the pair paid tribute to Yarman, opening Grandpa's Cheesebarn in Ashland, still its headquarters today. After selling their previous shop in 1991, the now namesake Grandma and Grandpa Baum came to work full time with the rest of the family, including fourth-generation Mistie Hray (Poorbaugh), who in 2015 expanded the family business to include two smaller footprint stores in Norton and Fairlawn under the moniker "Best of Grandpa's Cheesebarn."

But while the yellow "CHEESEBARN" sign beckons travelers to exit at US Highway 250 for the ever-popular cheese, jerky, jams and home smoked meats, those with a sweet tooth won't be sorry for stopping either. While the shop had long sold chocolates, it wasn't until 1995 that Ronda decided she would make homemade chocolates such as turtles and fudge on-site at the Ashland location, opening an additional store on the property and calling it "Sweetie's Chocolates." Using the highest quality of ingredients and made to Ronda's exacting standards, the team working in the dedicated chocolate room focuses on fresh batches of signature items made daily with love.

One such item is, of course, Sweetie's signature buckeye. Starting with a homemade peanut butter mix that is blended on-site, the staff hand rolls buckeye centers and then hand dips and packs them in six, twelve or twenty-four pieces. But the chocolate peanut butter deliciousness doesn't stop there at Sweetie's, as the buckeye takes center stage in everything from buckeye fudge to buckeye bark, M&M buckeye bites and even special

Sweetie's grew into its own separate building adjacent to Grandpa's Cheesebarn. *Grandpa's Cheesebarn.*

buckeye snack mix, featuring Sweetie's mini buckeye bites. Seasonally, the treat takes on a cooler side with buckeye ice cream, also used to make buckeye milkshakes.

And then there's the buckeye pizza. No, that's not a typo. Yes, they make a buckeye pizza, billed as "rich, flavorful and deliciously sweet!" There's no doubt that this crowd-pleasing, crew-feeding treat—which starts with a thick, rich base of Sweetie's signature milk chocolate topped generously with homemade mini buckeye candies, drizzled with white chocolate "sauce" and garnished with red and silver sparkle sprinkles—is a best-selling shop signature. Perfect for any Ohio State University tailgate or celebration, this unique sweet takes the buckeye love to another level.

Demand for buckeyes in all forms keeps Sweetie's employees busy, rolling buckeyes daily to keep up as guests come in to stock up. And customers visit Sweetie's from across the country (and world), recognizing their commitment to quality. One such instance is when at a trade show in Nevada in 2018, Sweetie's was instantly recognized because of their hand-rolled buckeyes.

A destination for both sweet and savory, Sweetie's Chocolates at Grandpa's Cheesebarn is a one-stop shop for all of your snacking needs. Centrally located an hour's drive from both Cleveland and Columbus, the Ashland flagship café offers sandwiches alongside samples of buckeye fudge and other treats seven days a week. Celebrating its forty-fifth year of carrying on the multi-generational dream dedicated to local, fresh, delicious products, the family says, "We only have plans to continue to expand and improve our stores, so come and enjoy a visit at Grandpa's Cheesebarn and Sweetie's Chocolates today!"

BELLBROOK CHOCOLATE SHOPPE

The great debate in the world of chocolate has long been whether milk or dark is "better." Whether that be from a strictly taste perspective or on the claims of healthfulness, the divide between milk chocolate lovers and dark chocolate enthusiasts can be intense, with both sides declaring their preference with conviction and pride. Betty Blose is Team Milk; her husband Byron was Team Dark.

As the founder of Bellbrook Chocolate Shoppe, Betty was faced with a dilemma during her first Easter in business in the spring of 1984: she wanted to make Easter eggs but knew some customers would want milk and others dark. When Byron suggested blending the two, Betty ran with the idea, experimenting with combining light (milk) and dark chocolate to create a taste they both enjoyed. Solving the Easter egg situation with a single signature offering, that blend has carried the company forward for going on four decades.

Betty had begun making chocolates in her home's second kitchen, a dedicated space downstairs, with plans to start a business with a friend. Original attempts were a struggle, so much so that the friend thought they should scratch the idea. But Betty's self-admitted stubbornness paid off as she committed herself to coming up with a buttercream recipe to mimic that of a candy shop she'd grown up going to as a child in Richmond, Indiana. Sheer determination combined with trial and error resulted in a product she was happy with and that friends had interest in giving as gifts. Next, a gift shop in town began selling her chocolates, and when a space opened next door, she decided to give opening her own shop a try under the moniker "Heavenly Hand Dipped Chocolates." Playing homage to the historic "Sheldonian" building's former life as an antique shop, Betty decorated with an old-fashioned theme, including her candy dish collection, now a family heirloom.

Exterior and interior of the current iteration of Betty Blose and family's Bellbrook Chocolate Shoppe in Centerville, Ohio. *Bellbrook Chocolate Shoppe.*

Dayton Daily News

FOOD

Lifestyle

WEDNESDAY, MARCH 31, 1999

hopping down the CHOCOLATE BUNNY *trail*

Taste testers have the sweet task of rating a hutch of Easter rabbits

By Ann Heller
DAYTON DAILY NEWS

Odds are you'll fill the kids' Easter baskets with hollow chocolate bunnies from the grocery store and discount store.

But a big, solid chocolate rabbit is more than a quick candy fix. It can be the center of the Easter dinner table display — and eventually a taste treat for those who are serious about their chocolate.

For a taste test of solid chocolate bunnies, we turned to confectioners scattered around Dayton. This week they'll be ringing up cash register sales for bunnies that weigh in from mere ounces to the 36-pound decorated rabbit available at Esther Price Candies for $242.

To check the quality of these bunnies, which are priced considerably higher than the hollow ones sold at chain stores, we invited seven chocoholics to evaluate them. We bought six solid-chocolate rabbits, and, out of curiosity, we included one inexpensive hollow rabbit from a chain.

In the blind tasting, the decisive winner for the panelists was the chocolate rabbit from Bellbrook Chocolate Shoppe, which just moved from Bellbrook to Cross Pointe Centre in Centerville.

That bunny, made from the house blend of both milk and dark chocolate, was the first-place choice of five of the tasters. All the others in the tasting were pure milk chocolate.

In second place was the bunny from Esther Price, a name synonymous with chocolate in Dayton. It wasn't a uniform judgment, though. One Esther Price fan, who was sure she would recognize it, labeled it "Just OK." Panelists, who weren't told the cost of the bunnies, might have been more impressed if they'd realized the prices on the Dayton leader were cheaper than the others in the competition.

A number of panelists noted similar tastes in bunnies from Esther Price, Nurrenbrock Quality Candies and Friesinger's candies, a taste and aroma they said reminded them of the chocolate bunnies of their childhood.

SEE BUNNIES/2C

RABBIT TEST

JIM WITMER
DAYTON DAILY NEWS

Panelists rated bunnies on a 1-to-10 scale. Here's how items fared based on average scores:

▶ **1. Bellbrook Chocolate Shoppe,** Cross Pointe Centre, Centerville, 7.5-ounce bunny, $6.50. **Rating:** 7.7.

▶ **2. Esther Price Candies,** 1709 Wayne Ave., 1-pound bunny, $7.95. **Rating:** 6.6.

▶ **3. Nurrenbrock Quality Candies,** 2570 Shiloh Springs Road, Trotwood, 1-pound, 3-ounce bunny, $11.94. **Rating:** 6.0.

▶ **4. Candy Garden,** 9338 S. Main St., Centerville, 12-ounce bunny, $9. **Rating:** 5.9.

▶ **5. Friesinger's Candies,** 45 N. Pioneer Blvd., off Ohio 73, Springboro, 1-pound bunny, $11.95. **Rating:** 5.1.

▶ **6. Winans Fine Chocolates,** 10 N. Main St., Troy, 13.5-ounce bunny, $11.35. **Rating:** 3.5.

▶ **7. Meijer Supermarket,** 4075 Wilmington Pike, Kettering, hollow 5-ounce bunny, $2.59 (made by R.M. Palmer Co. West Reading, Pa.). **Rating:** 2.

BUNNIES: Tasters rate chocolate rabbits

CONTINUED FROM/1C

Another rabbit, from Centerville's Candy Garden, got mixed reviews. Two panelists gave it first-place marks, but three rated it unacceptable. Five tasters also rated a bunny from Winans Fine Chocolates in Troy as unacceptable, complaining of a "strange"or "off" flavor.

The panelists were uniform in their distaste for the national-brand chocolate bunny purchased at Meijer. All but one rated it unacceptable — and two spit out the chocolate.

The bunnies were similar but not identical. They ranged in size from the 7.5-ounce flat bunny from Bellbrook Chocolates to a hefty 1 pound, 3 ounce specimen from Nurrenbrock. The list of ingredients on the four that provided labels were virtually identical: milk chocolate, sugar,

whole milk, cocoa butter and chocolate liquor. The labels all listed lecithin, an emulsifier, and vanillin, an artificial flavoring.

Most are poured into commercial plastic molds, explaining their look-alike appearances, but we were told that at Friesinger Candies the rabbits are hand-molded in antique metal molds, rather than plastic.

Looks counted in the rating,

but we were mostly interested in taste. So we told our judges to take a bite, place it on the tongue and lift it to slowly melt. That's the way serious chocolate eaters check the quality.

Note that while we used milk chocolate because that is America's favorite chocolate, many of the stores offer the bunnies in dark or white chocolate as well.

The *Dayton Daily News* ranked Bellbrook Chocolate Shoppe's chocolate bunny number one for Easter 1999, just one week after the store opened in its new location. *Bellbrook Chocolate Shoppe.*

A year later, when the opportunity to move across the street arose, Betty purchased the historic building at the main intersection in downtown Bellbrook with a friend and renamed her business the more marketable "Bellbrook Chocolates." With a storied history, the building formerly

A sweetly wrapped buckeye-supporting shortbread cookie, another signature of Bellbrook Chocolate Shoppe. *Bellbrook Chocolate Shoppe.*

housed a grocer, post office and namesake Barnett's of Bellbrook furniture store. Betty and her friend initially leased out space for smaller gift shops in a boutique fashion, and after she and Byron became the sole owners of the building in 1986, she grew what became known as the Bellbrook Village Shoppes. With a range of offerings from country-inspired and upscale gifts (crystal, brass, china, etc.) as well as gourmet foods, a Christmas loft and art gallery, Betty oversaw its successful operation for thirteen years until the spring of 1999. It was at that time that she wanted to focus solely on her "chocolate roots" and sold the building and moved to a more suitable location in Centerville with a newer retail space and production kitchen she designed herself. But even though she'd crossed town lines, she kept the Bellbrook name, which had become well known in the wider Dayton area after being voted number one chocolate rabbit in a blind taste test by the *Dayton Daily News* just one week after the company opened in its new location. "It was also four days before Easter," she recalls, and says they "could barely keep up with the rabbit orders!"

Shortly after moving the shop to Centerville, Betty welcomed her son, Marshall; daughter-in-law, Laura; and their then four-year-old daughter, Emily, back to the area to join her in the family business. Though it was quite a transition from their previous work in the Thoroughbred horse world in Kentucky, Marshall had experience helping his mom make candy many times during holiday visits, and Laura had already begun baking shortbread cookies for Betty's business while living in Lexington. Now known as "Aunt Laura's Shortbread Cookies," they've become a signature staple of Bellbrook's offering, available as an assortment, Linzer style (sandwiched with seedless black raspberry jam), decorated for holidays and, of course, dipped in chocolate.

Laura's cookies are one of two reasons the shop has a commercial convection oven—the other being another signature offering, sugared praline pecans and cinnamon sugar almonds—while the only other "machines" in Bellbrook's Candy Kitchen are two pots that melt and temper chocolate and a microwave tthat warms the bowls before they're filled with chocolate. Each item is handmade, hand rolled or cut and individually dipped in bowls of

Chocolate covered-strawberries and the Bellbrook pretzel, two specialty items with an extra-special mission: a portion of proceeds from each item supports a local breast cancer foundation. *Bellbrook Chocolate Shoppe.*

the signature blend of light and dark chocolate, with no added preservatives. "After thirty-eight years in business, and the growth that we have seen, the chocolate is still made just as it was originally in my home candy kitchen," says Betty proudly.

Among those labors of love are offerings from creams, caramels, nuts and chews, including Betty's favorite, her peanut cream cluster. Originally created in likeness to the Old-Fashioned Bunn Candy Bar, it consists of buttercream on the bottom and chocolate peanuts on top. While son Marshall's go-to is his namesake, Marshall's Favorite (a combination of chocolate, peanuts and toffee), Laura's is a decadently famous offering dedicated to the shop's moniker, the Bellbrook Pretzel (a pretzel rod dipped in caramel, rolled in toffee chips and then dipped in either their signature blend chocolate or signature white blend). Beyond delicious, the Bellbrook Pretzel also gives back, joining forces with a seasonal specialty, double-dipped strawberries (dipped first in the Signature White Chocolate Blend and then in the Signature Blend), dipped fresh each morning from late January through the end of October. Each year, a portion of proceeds from these two items is donated to a local breast cancer foundation.

When it comes to buckeyes, not only are Bellbrook's distinct due to their signature blend, but they also make their own peanut butter cream from scratch. Marshall's the main man making this Ohio tradition, and he rolls out each individual buckeye ball and then dips each one in the shop's signature blend chocolate, with no machines involved. In fact, he prides himself on his telltale handmade sign, the small hole on top of each buckeye that comes from the cake tester he uses to hold the peanut butter ball as he's dipping

Whether in trays or two packs, the Bellbrook Chocolate Shoppe buckeye is great for gatherings. *Bellbrook Chocolate Shoppe.*

it in chocolate. Laura recalls someone once asking why he didn't cover up each little hole and Marshall replying, "Why would I do that? It's the hole that proves they're hand dipped!" Bellbrook's buckeyes are available year-round but become an even bigger bestseller during the busy seasons of OSU football and Christmas. Just this fall, Laura encountered a customer with a self-proclaimed "Buckeye Emergency," a last-minute order for a quantity of 140 by noon the same day. Marshall made it happen, nearly averting a buckeye candy catastrophe.

Left: A sweet setup behind the scenes at Bellbrook Chocolate Shoppe's annual "All You Can Eat Chocolate Party." *Bellbrook Chocolate Shoppe.*

Opposite: Bellbrook Chocolate Shoppe's second location inside of downtown Dayton's Second Street Market. *Bellbrook Chocolate Shoppe.*

The family is familiar with large quantities of candy, annually hosting an "All You Can Eat Chocolate Party," for the past twenty years. Inviting customers into their candy kitchen each September, the ticketed event grants behind-the-scenes access to see where "all the magic happens," says Laura, while enjoying tastes of over eighty-seven items. From the classics like creams and caramels, fudge, sugared nuts and, of course, her signature shortbread cookies to novelties including chocolate-dipped Oreos, grahams and strawberries, she adds, "It's just about everything we make!"

In addition to the Centerville shop, Bellbrook Chocolates has a booth at the Second Street Market in downtown Dayton, which is open weekends (Friday/Saturday/Sunday) year-round. Housed in a renovated train depot at the corner of Second and Webster, vendors offer everything from fruits/vegetables, locally/ethically raised beef, olive oils, handmade soaps, fresh

baked bread, hand thrown pottery, jewelry, delicious food such as crepes to order and, of course, chocolate! Laura loves this area for its many museums (National Museum of the U.S. Air Force, Boonschoft Children's Museum, The Packard Museum, the International Peace Museum), Carillon Historical Park and the Dayton Dragons, the minor league baseball team that holds the all-time sellout record for sports franchises in

BELLBROOK'S OTHER SIGNATURE: SHORTBREAD

From Thanksgiving turkeys to colorfully swirled fall leaves, smiley faces to sailboats, butterflies to buckeyes (the OSU kind), Laura's custom cookies are works of art, with taste to match. Everyone in the family has their favorite, even the baker herself:

- Marshall: Aunt Laura's White Chocolate Toffee Shortbread Cookies
- Laura: Aunt Laura's Almond Shortbread Cookies
- Emily: Chocolate-Dipped Aunt Laura's (Mom's) Butter Shortbread

North America. "Basically, whatever you enjoy, you most likely can find it here or close to us," she says, adding, "Many people move here because of the base [Wright-Patterson Air Force] and end up retiring here because they love the area!"

If you can't make the trip though, not to worry; Bellbrook ships across the country as well as internationally. "We have personally shipped our chocolate as far as Canada, Germany, and Japan and we know our customers have taken it as far as places in Europe, Asia and South America," says Laura, with a note specific to sharing Ohio's signature sweet: "We love it when people take buckeyes to different states and countries and explain what it is and where it comes from." For her part, Laura loves educating those who aren't familiar with the namesake nut, keeping a jar of real buckeyes at the shop for "show and tell," especially for visitors touring the Buckeye Candy Trail.

Ecstatic to have built a business for the next generation to carry on, Betty says, "It has been so satisfying to see the growth that has occurred through the efforts of two generations." And she has high hopes that the legacy will continue, adding, "My granddaughter Emily grew up in the Chocolate Shoppe and even though she is grown and has a career of her own, she maintains an interest and is very proud of the family business. Who knows what the future will bring!" With the perfect balance of Betty's Signature Chocolate Blend, whatever comes next for Bellbrook Chocolate Shoppe is sure to be sweet.

Candy Cottage

Many businesses are passed down generationally, but few can say they've created a family by linking together five female owners, as is the case for the Candy Cottage in Lancaster. Originally opened in the 1960s by Florence Stotler, it was subsequently led by Barb Smelzer, Norma Franco, Lisa Morris and current proprietor Alice DuBois, who has been at the helm since 2008. Of this forged bond between the women who have carried its legacy through the decades, Alice remarks, "I love each one of the ladies that owned Candy Cottage. I'm so proud to be a part of this community's past and present," adding, "each of us inspiring creative and delicious treats for our community. Each having their own unique style and recipes to add to our amazing history of delightful bites."

For her part, Alice has carried on the tradition of focusing on fresh, quality products and personalized service. She leverages recipes dating back to the shop's opening, some of which, such as the handmade butter creams, are still made using the original chocolate molds. She also retained some of the shop's original glassware, even after a relocation in 2015. While moving brought the typically involved challenges, Alice credits the opportunity to broadening the shop's client base, including easier access for those with mobility issues, additional parking and proximity to neighboring areas of Pickerington and Canal Winchester. The new space also allowed her to expand her offering to include bakery items, espresso and cold brew, perfect complements to the existing selection of sweets.

Candy Cottage's fifth fearless female leader, Alice DuBois. *Candy Cottage.*

And those sweets draw customers both old and new, with over thirty-five varieties handmade in house in small batches from haystacks to heath bars, caramels to cherries, creams to clusters. Gourmet pretzels, barks and specialty mints complement the offering, as well as a long list of panned products including chocolate-covered nuts, raisins, malt balls and coffee beans.

Another signature offering, Alice roasts redskin peanuts every Tuesday, a favorite of local clubs and golf courses.

But of course, it's the best-selling buckeye that's a fan favorite not only on its own but incorporated into the shop's bakery case atop cupcakes and brownies as well as at the coffee counter, featured in the Buckeye Bliss offering. Though Alice says the shop's recipe is quite typical, she credits a combination of the blend of brands used and the fact that they're made in small batches, hand rolled, hand dipped and—likely the secret—mixed with love by "an amazing team that loves their job." Whatever the reason, the Candy Cottage's process is certainly working, as she adds that keeping them in stock is a labor of love. "It's a never-ending, three-to-four-days-a-week job. We sell so many it's wonderful!" And word has spread, with customers sharing this Ohio original all over

A towering trio of signature buckeye candies from Lancaster's long-standing Candy Cottage. *K Rodenbaugh.*

the world, including Germany, Australia, New Zealand and many military bases. A highlight achievement of the business was having the opportunity to supply gifts to Congress and the National Republican Party, as no matter your political preferences, Alice says, "It's neat to hear Steve Stivers talk about your product and ask people to please support our business. Pretty cool, right?"

Though buckeyes will always be top of mind for Alice, she says her personal favorite treat fluctuates day by day and that "after making them and eating them for so many years, I've moved on to the peanut clusters with caramel center. Yum!" Additional bestsellers include turtles, lemon and pecan pie bars and, on the other side of the house, the Chai and Pay Day espresso drinks. The shop also receives a variety of custom orders, from corporate gift baskets to specialty items for weddings, baby showers, open houses and trade shows, all tailored to the event theme.

When asked if she always saw herself in the candy business, Alice laughs (she left a career in the computer industry to take over the Candy Cottage), saying that though her current involvement started as more of a stress relief to offset her full-time job, making candy has been a part of her life since grade school. "When I was a young girl, my best friend Denise and I were joined at the hip. Her brother Jerry was in the Boy Scouts and was learning how to make candy. So, he let us learn at the same time," adding that the pair took their venture to the next level, becoming youthful entrepreneurs. "Denise and I would make suckers and treats and sell them that year on the school bus and at lunch. We had so much fun making them together." She also recalls making giant gingerbread houses with Diane's dad to take to a nearby nursing home, recalling the joy it brought to residents.

Fast-forward a few years to Alice working nearly a full-time second job to create candy, cookies and cakes for friends and family, remembering how much she enjoyed the creativity involved in the process. With the support of her husband and two children, she left her previous career to pursue this lifelong love and embraced the opportunity to also teach others. The shop caters to home bakers by carrying candy melts as well as both candy and cake-making supplies such as molds, colorings and decorations. Alice and her knowledgeable team are always available to answer questions and have the ability to show customers what items are used for what purposes and how to use them. Summing up their support of those learning to love the business as much as she does, Alice says, "We enjoy hearing about your candy successes and your families' traditions in candy making."

While both the move and the more recent COVID-19 pandemic top her list of business challenges, Alice continues to shepherd the Candy Cottage through times of change and uncertainty with grace and dedication. She credits the support of her team, customers and landlord with surviving the latter, saying that while it was certainly a stressful time, in the end it deepened existing relationships and strengthened the already strong sense of community. Customers called with concern and kind words, came out to say they didn't necessarily need anything but wanted to help and even offered tips for the team, which had previously never been taken but became a major source of support and brought joy to the small team still working in the business. "To say that we have the best customers and team is an understatement. We didn't make money, but we got to stay in business because our customers demanded it," says Alice. She also credits the building's landlord, adding, "I have the most incredible landlord. Before things got tight, he reached out and said, 'We are here. We will help you get through this!' Who does that? It's unexpected and wonderful!" Though the business is still recovering from challenges such as closures and product sourcing, Alice is thankful for what they retained and gained, in respect to customer commitment and community connectedness.

As she continues to bounce back, Alice looks toward the future of the Candy Cottage, balancing the legacy she's proud to carry on with fresh opportunities such as collaborations with local brewery Double Edge Brewing Co., co-promotion of neighboring massage business Elements of Health and even in-store live music for special events such as Small Business Saturday. Social promotions, a Chocolate of the Month Club and support of local charities such as the Fairfield Center for disAbilities and Cerebral Palsy also play a part in how the business continues its longtime connection with customers and the surrounding community. While Alice acknowledges that competition from big-box stores brings challenges for small businesses in the specialty goods space, she believes a focus on the customer and product quality will allow the Candy Cottage to stay strong for generations to come.

THE ORIGINAL GOODIE SHOP

The Original Goodie Shop doesn't make fortune cookies, but its business may have been saved by the message in one: "Take the initiative and others will support you." Owner Debbie Smith has carried this mantra with her since 2009, when she and her daughters, co-owners Emilie and Miranda, brought her father's shop back to life through the support of their Upper Arlington (UA) community. While this iteration of the bakery's life is led by a force of female family members, its origins start with a band of brothers, quite literally those of Debbie's father, Jim Krenek.

The youngest of twelve children born to Czechoslovakian parents, Jim and his siblings grew up watching their mother cook and bake for the large family. After the passing of his father when he was only nine years old, times were tight, and oldest brother Joe opened a small bakery named the Neighborhood Bakery in German Village. Wanting to also support his mother financially, Jim enlisted in the navy at age seventeen, lying about his age to gain acceptance, and requested that he be assigned to cook and bakers school. He was eventually assigned aboard USS *Saratoga*, a navy aircraft carrier. Learning the skills of the trade cooking and baking for the 2,200 crewmen aboard the ship, Jim served from 1944 on, including after World War II, when the ship instead transported army and navy personnel back and forth from Hawaii to San Diego. After his navy discharge, Jim joined his brothers at Joe's Neighborhood Bakery until Joe's sudden passing, at which time the brothers closed up shop. Looking for another location, brothers John, Stanley, Bryan and Jim started the Kenmore Bakery in a building attached to the Kenmore Grocery Store. There they built a successful business while another brother, Frank, started a bakery just outside Columbus, in Marysville. Baking was certainly in the blood of the Krenek family.

While on his bakery sales route, Jim met Bill Wood, original owner of the Tremont Goodie Shop, opened in 1955 in the neighborhood of Upper Arlington. After twelve years in business, Wood was looking to sell the shop and mentioned it to Jim, who expressed interest. Upon purchasing the bakery, Jim employed a staff of about twelve people, including hiring his own daughter Debbie starting when she was just a junior in high school. Recalling working six days a week, Debbie had plans to attend college and pursue a teaching career when her father asked her to consider managing another bakery he wanted to purchase in a different UA shopping center. She accepted, and the quality reputation of both bakeries continued to grow, as Jim started yet a third bakery and bought a truck to drive daily between the three. Once brought on board as partner and cake decorator, respectively, Debbie's younger brother and older sister both left the family business for other jobs, causing the increased workload of managing three bakeries to be too much. After selling two of the three bakeries, one to a former employee, the original bakery remained at its primary location, but future challenges still befell the family.

In 2006, Debbie had become the primary caregiver for both Jim and her mother, MaryEllen, whose health was declining. As she was also raising her own family of three children with her husband, Don, managing the bakery became difficult, and she eventually made the decision to give the bakery to her older sister and brother-in-law. Hoping to keep the bakery in business both for her family as well as the employees who had become friends, if not equally like family, Debbie continued to work at the shop part time until differences in management style caused her to cease involvement. Likewise, many longtime employees also sought employment elsewhere after Debbie's departure.

But in July 2009, Debbie was contacted by the owners of the shopping center asking if she would resume management of the bakery's operations, as her sister and brother-in-law had fallen behind on rent. Not wanting to push them out of the business, she initially declined, until that September, when she got a call from a former employee telling her that the bakery had closed; the windows were papered over, and a large sign indicated, "Due to the economy, the bakery is closed." Equally as shocked as Debbie herself were the bakery's loyal customers, who were nearly in mourning, with some even laying flowers outside the storefront. After the shopping center's owners again reached out to her asking if she could reopen the bakery, Debbie contacted her brother-in-law, asking if he'd be willing to give it back to her, as she had given it to him. He declined, indicating she would have to attend the auction for the business and its assets. Disappointed but not deterred, Debbie decided to talk to her daughters, Emilie and Miranda, both recent college grads looking for jobs.

The three met for dinner at a favorite local Chinese restaurant to discuss whether they should reopen the bakery. Though her father had passed away, both Debbie and her daughters felt strongly about carrying on his legacy, as both of them fondly recalled helping out at the bakery while in high school. To sum up the meal, and their conversation, fortune cookies arrived, and Emilie and Miranda urged their mother to choose the first one. Upon opening it, Debbie recalls getting choked up as she attempted to read her fortune aloud, finally getting out the motivating message meant just for that exact moment: "Take the initiative, and others will support you."

Taking the sign seriously, Emilie and Miranda jumped into the campaign, starting a Facebook page dedicated to "Save the Goodie Shop." Daily they reported back numbers of new supporters to Debbie, reading stories shared by customers of their favorite memories of the beloved bakery. The following grew fast, with fans asking how else they could support the endeavor, even asking Debbie to open an account at the bank for them to contribute donations directly. To further their efforts, Emilie and Miranda suggested they design T-shirts, originally for the family to wear to the auction. When they found out there was a minimum order quantity of one dozen, they posted the shirt design (a white shirt with "I (red heart) the Goodie Shop") to the Facebook page to determine interest from supporters and within a week had over four hundred orders.

Auction day came, and Debbie was greeted by not only her immediate family but also former employees, who had become friends, their families and fans wearing the Goodie Shop T-shirts. To further boost morale, Emilie and Miranda had baked a signature Goodie Shop cookie recipe and were offering them free of charge to customers who came out in support. Initially scared and upset by the sight of both the number of other bidders as well as the bakery, which had been emptied by the auction company, Debbie buckled down to begin bidding but realized quickly she wasn't going it alone. As former bakery customers approached her asking

Two longtime employees, Phyllis Fankhouser and Hazel Grooms, behind the counter at the Goodie Shop. *The Original Goodie Shop.*

which items she needed, they indicated they were going to bid on those items and asked where they'd like her to stack them once secured. With tears of gratitude flowing, Debbie focused on purchasing only the items required to reopen but was stunned again when the auctioneer indicated he would begin the sale of the large equipment inside the bakery. Fearful she couldn't be in both places at the same time, Debbie's team of previous employees stepped in, assuring her they knew what was of necessity and would stay outside to bid on the smaller items.

While inside, one of those employees came to tell Debbie that the owners of other bakeries had begun asking them about the auction's backstory. Once they heard why the auction was being held, they indicated they would not bid against her if she bid first. With this small relief, Debbie and her supporters made it to the end of the day feeling hopeful—until the purchases were added up by the auction house. She recalls the panic that set in when the auctioneer said she had to pay for everything that day, saying, "I had an available line of credit second mortgage on our home, and every last

OHIO SENATE

HONORING
THE ORIGINAL GOODIE SHOP
FOR EXCEPTIONAL ACHIEVEMENT

On behalf of the members of the Senate of the 128th General Assembly of Ohio, we are pleased to extend special recognition to The Original Goodie Shop on being named the 2009 Business of the Year by the Upper Arlington Area Chamber of Commerce.

This prestigious honor is a fitting tribute to The Original Goodie Shop, for its employees have consistently demonstrated professionalism and expertise, as well as a commitment to maintaining the highest quality standards. Due to the exemplary effort and initiative its staff has displayed, the business has attained a tremendous record of service to the community, and this noteworthy enterprise is truly deserving of high praise.

The accomplishments of The Original Goodie Shop are a justifiable source of pride and an outstanding reflection not only on the enterprise itself but also on its owner, Debbie Krenek, on its hard-working employees, and on the community. The venture has enhanced the quality of life within the surrounding area, and we are certain that in the years to come, this fine establishment will continue to display the same unwavering dedication to excellence for which it has become known.

Thus, with sincere pleasure, we commend The Original Goodie Shop on its recent accolade and extend best wishes for ongoing success.

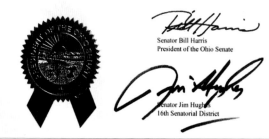

Senator Bill Harris
President of the Ohio Senate

Senator Jim Hughes
16th Senatorial District

The official proclamation recognizing the Original Goodie Shop as a 2009 Business of the Year by the Ohio Senate after its grand reopening. *The Original Goodie Shop.*

penny of the credit line was spent…[but] I was short of money." Coming to her rescue, Emilie and Miranda tallied the total from their rally table, where supporters had come to purchase their reserved T-shirts and made additional cash donations. In another stroke of resilience, they had exactly the right amount of money to clear Debbie's debt.

Surrounded by supporters, Debbie, her family and the former employees carried everything purchased back into the bakery. A team of loyalists whom Debbie dubbed her "Dream Team" came daily for weeks following the auction to clean, organize and make the repairs required to reopen. Within

OHIO SENATE

HONORING
THE TREMONT GOODIE SHOP
ON ITS RE-OPENING

On behalf of the members of the Senate of the 128th General Assembly of Ohio, we are pleased to congratulate the Tremont Goodie Shop on the memorable occasion of its grand re-opening, October 26, 2009.

Recognition of this special event is a fitting tribute to the Tremont Goodie Shop, for it has achieved a remarkable record of service to the Greater Columbus area. The store has earned the gratitude and appreciation of many satisfied customers, and its success is a justifiable source of pride and an outstanding reflection not only on the business itself but also on its astute management, on its hard-working employees, and on the community.

Over the years, the Tremont Goodie Shop has enhanced the quality of life within the surrounding area, and it is truly deserving of high praise. We are certain that as this worthy enterprise maintains its dedication to service, it will continue to grow and prosper and will follow in the tradition of excellence that has become its hallmark.

Thus, with sincere pleasure, we commend the Tremont Goodie Shop on its re-opening and extend best wishes for the future.

Senator Bill Harris
President of the Ohio Senate

Senator Jim Hughes
16th Senatorial District

The official proclamation recognizing the Original Goodie Shop's reopening by the Ohio Senate. *The Original Goodie Shop.*

just one month, on October 26, 2009, Debbie's dedicated crew cut the ribbon on the grand reopening under the new moniker, the Original Goodie Shop. Welcoming back customers, the team baked 1,200 each of their signature smile cookies and famous cinnamon sticks to give away to those in attendance, including the mayor of Upper Arlington, who had issued a proclamation declaring it the Goodie Shop Week. The accolades went even further, all the way up to the statehouse in fact, when Ohio representative Jim Hughes signed and presented the bakery with a congratulatory edict. And hometown happiness extended from individuals sending the bakery

CITY OF **UPPER ARLINGTON**
OFFICE OF THE MAYOR

Proclamation

THE ORIGINAL GOODIE SHOP WEEK

WHEREAS, the City of Upper Arlington values the contributions of locally owned and operated businesses, not only for the economic stability they bring, but also for their contribution to the quality of life within the community; and

WHEREAS, in 1955, The Tremont Goodie Shop opened its doors for business and for these many years has been an integral part of the continued enjoyment, growth and prosperity of our community; and

WHEREAS, for more than 50 years The Tremont Goodie Shop offered a true, old-fashioned bakery loved by residents of our community; and

WHEREAS, the sudden and unanticipated closure of the Shop reminded us all of the importance of patronizing and supporting the locally owned businesses that we value so much; and

WHEREAS, because of the committed and tireless efforts of Debbie Smith, her family and the many friends and fans of the Goodie Shop who donated their time and support, this icon of Upper Arlington has reopened as of October 24, 2009 as The Original Goodie Shop;

NOW, THEREFORE, I, Donald B. Leach Jr., Mayor of the City of Upper Arlington, do hereby extend my personal congratulations to The Original Goodie Shop, and proclaim the week of October 25 to October 31, 2009 as

The Original Goodie Shop Week

and urge all citizens to join in recognition and celebration of this locally owned business, its welcomed return and the vital role it has and will play in our community.

IN WITNESS WHEREOF, I have hereunto set my hand and caused the Seal of the City of Upper Arlington, Ohio, to be affixed this 26th day of October 2009.

Mayor

The official proclamation from the City of Upper Arlington declaring the week of October 25 to 31, 2009, as the Original Goodie Shop Week in celebration of the shop's reopening. *The Original Goodie Shop.*

letters, flowers and balloons as well as posting heartfelt messages on the shop's Facebook page, which had exploded with followers since inception. To sum up the support, that year the Upper Arlington Chamber of Commerce voted the bakery "Business of the Year."

Back in business, Debbie, her daughters and their team focused on longtime fan favorites, like the aforementioned cinnamon sticks. A signature shop item, they consist of four thin layers of sweet roll dough, with cinnamon and sugar sandwiched between each layer, all topped off with gooey butterscotch. Each tray of ten dozen takes a practiced baker at least twenty minutes to assemble. Once baked, they are cut into one-by-three-inch rectangles. Debbie describes, "The best part of a cinnamon roll—the very center that is oh so good." Customers couldn't agree more, gobbling up 130,000 in 2021 and on track for similar in 2022. She adds that they're "ideal for shipping and have been sent to all over the world—even to Afghanistan and Guantanamo Bay to give a 'little taste of home' to servicemen." Butter cookies, cut out and decorated to match any occasion, are another bestseller, with the shop's smile cookie leading the pack year-round. Opting for a soft frosting and decorations over a harder, fondant-type frosting sets this signature apart, as do the exclusive rights from The Ohio State University to use licensed OSU images. The total for cutout cookies in 2021 was 71,000, which Debbie declared as "an amazing amount for a small bakery!"

The connection to buckeyes, both lowercase and capital *B*, extends to another of the shop's signature recipes developed by Debbie's dad. Dating back to the 1960s, Jim caught on to the craze quickly, perfecting his version to be, as Debbie describes them today, "creamy, not gritty, and coated in dark chocolate, which adds to the flavor, instead of milk chocolate, which is much milder in flavor." Another distinction comes down on the "prettier" side of the debate, with Debbie adding, "The Goodie Shop's buckeyes do not have the unsightly toothpick hole in the middle of each one either. Best of all, they do look like a real buckeye!" As such, the Goodie Shop's buckeyes were voted among the ten best in Ohio by *USA Today* in 2019. While the company's editors selected the top twenty, a popular vote chose the final ten.

The Goodie Shop decorates buckeyes for all occasions, from Easter's Bucky buckeye bunnies to reindeer, angels and Santa faces at Christmas, festive hats for Mother's Day, wedding veils and suits/ties for brides and grooms, respectively. (One couple even requested two giant buckeyes, a bride and groom, to be placed on top of their wedding cake!) But the most popular are the eponymously decorated OSU Buckeyes wearing hats in their iconic school colors, scarlet and gray. They've traveled across state lines, with customers buying boxes to take to family and friends in other states, especially those who Debbie says "want to 'rub it in' when visiting Michigan fans!" For fans of both the team and treat, no better birthday cake exists than Debbie's popular design, which uses four buckeye candies lined up on the edge of a sheet cake with stick arms and legs on each to pose them as a letter spelling O-H-I-O, similar to how the university's marching band famously spells the word in script while performing on its football field. Again, licensed exclusively, this cake is only available at the Original Goodie Shop.

One of the shop's other cake creations earned top billing when Debbie was put on the spot to pick her personal favorite. She recalls, "I was once asked by the local newspaper reporter what my most favorite item was. I was taken aback because I had never been asked that before. As I scanned the showcases, there were cinnamon sticks, cream horns, donuts, cookies—how to decide?!" But then she spotted it: a two-layer white cake made following the same recipe her father developed the same year he bought the shop, 1967, and iced with his white buttercream icing recipe from around the same time. As soon as her eyes landed on this nostalgic choice, she knew it was the one, saying, "I still have to indulge in our white cake for special occasions."

As a full line shop, the list of delights continues from cream horns—hand rolled from French pastry dough, folded, cut, molded and finally filled with a made-from-scratch buttercream and sprinkled with powdered sugar—to donuts, especially a chocolate-iced, custard-filled variety that one customer loves so much he once paid $1,000 for a single one. Carroll Mobley, a longtime UA resident who has frequented the Goodie Shop for over a decade, called one day during the COVID-19 pandemic to ask for his favorite donut to be saved for him. When he arrived to pick it up, he asked for Emilie and told her he had received his government stimulus check but did not really need the money. Considering where he could donate it to be of help, he offered her roughly nine hundred times the price of the pastry, which is typically $1.10. He told her he wanted to make sure the bakery stayed in business and to use it where she needed it most. Little did Mr. Mobley know that his generous gesture would be picked up both by the national news, as a feature narrated by Lester Holt on NBC's *Today Show*, as well as subsequently in a book by fellow anchor Hoda Kotb. About a year after the TV segment, Kotb's book featuring an uplifting story for each day of the year was released, dedicating January 6 to the Original Goodie Shop. The bakery's Facebook page went wild with messages from those who had read the tale, though none of the shop's staff knew their story had been included. Kotb's personal post for the day expressed her emotional reaction to the story, saying, "I've never gotten choked up about a doughnut. Doughnuts make me happy! But I teared up when *Today* aired a story about an act of kindness that unfolded for an Ohio bakery owner."

Likewise, Debbie's dedication runs deep, with the shop participating in a variety of events throughout the year, including the Golden Bear Bash, which supports the Educational Foundation for Upper Arlington schools; the Night of Chocolate and Kitchen Kapers, both of which support cancer communities; Zoofari, a fundraiser for the Columbus Zoo; and both the Columbus Coffee Fest and Donut and Beer Fest. The bakery also makes cutout cookies for charitable causes such as pink ribbon cookies for breast cancer and donates a percentage of sales of cinnamon sticks to support ALS research.

Free Treats for First-Timers and Trick-or-Treaters

Even if you visit the Original Goodie Shop as a stop on the Ohio Buckeye Candy Trail, it's quite likely you'll be tempted by the myriad other treats. If you're a first-time visitor (Debbie says the staff can spot them because of the overwhelmed look most people get as they *ooh* and *ahh* over all the options), the shop's signature promotion is to treat you to a free cinnamon stick, which "are always well received and appreciated—and practically guarantee they become repeat customers!"

For the bakery's younger clientele, a stop in the shopping center during its annual Halloween parade (which brings approximately eight hundred children combined between the nearby public and Catholic elementary schools) gets each child a coupon to choose a donut on their next visit. Whether they wait until the night's candy has been depleted or double down the next day is a decision Debbie leaves to their parents, though if the kids had their way, it would of course be the latter.

Connected to the community that continues to carry it through ups and downs, Debbie believes in the future of the Original Goodie Shop, saying it "has and will continue to stand the test of time." Challenges in the confectionary industry certainly exist, and the last few years have been no exception, though the bakery was able to weather the pandemic without decline in large part due to Ohio's governor declaring bakeries essential during early pandemic business closures. In addition to Mr. Mobley's support, Debbie says, "It is as if the customers remembered what happened in 2009, and they were determined to keep the bakery in business for many years to come." With increasing year after year sales and the talents brought by third-generation owners, Emilie managing day-to-day operations and Miranda as the master cake decorator, Debbie envisions the Original Goodie Shop serving Upper Arlington residents (and those who come from all over Ohio to visit) long into the future, even expanding in its existing space if/when possible. She's supported by a staff of now twenty to twenty-five employees who, like their customers, couldn't be happier that Debbie decided to follow her fortune and "take the initiative."

TICKLED SWEET

Equal parts entrepreneur and chocolate lover, Bambi Merz has a sharp eye for both business and buckeyes. An executive coach by trade, Bambi somewhat stumbled into the sweet side of things roughly ten years ago, while on business at one of the largest candy and snack expos in the world. At the time unaware how intimately involved in the industry she would become, her passion for both confections and creativity led her down a new path, as she recalls feeling like the proverbial "kid in a candy store...mesmerized by the atmosphere."

Saying the samples kept her coming back year after year, Bambi's return to the expo would, five years in, connect her with Randy Auel of Auel's Fine Chocolates. A quick study, Bambi learned the tricks of the trade behind delicious treats by helping out at Auel's store. Ready to relinquish the reins, Randy spent multiple months teaching Bambi recipes that had been passed down through generations of his family. Taking over ownership in 2016, Bambi carried on Auel's legacy while crafting her own confections, all still handmade, hand rolled and hand dipped. From fondant centers dipped in milk, dark or white chocolate to favorites such as sea salt caramels and deluxe turtles, customer favorites haven't changed even as Bambi rebranded to Tickled Sweet.

In addition to the rebrand, Bambi found a new home for her new business just four months after acquiring Auel's. A former printing company, the building in downtown Historic Milford had been purchased at auction, and just days after finding it, Bambi had a handshake deal to make it hers. The transformation was almost as quick, taking a dedicated crew less than two months to build out a beautiful retail space as well as a full kitchen, production and shipping areas. Designed with customers in mind, Bambi laid out the shop to showcase its variety of offerings, including signature specialties such her personal favorite, the dark chocolate–dipped opera cream truffle. "It's a simple piece, but the dark chocolate is exceptional, and the opera cream center blends wonderfully with the dark chocolate," Bambi describes.

Similarly, "simple" but deceivingly delicious are Bambi's buckeyes. Disclosing what she calls the "secret" ingredient, she starts with Jif peanut butter and then adds the rest of the usual suspects. Like all of her artisanal chocolates, the buckeyes are handmade, with the centers hand rolled

The exterior of Tickled Sweet in its new location in downtown Milford, Ohio. *Tickled Sweet.*

Tickled Sweet's assortment of treats. *Tickled Sweet.*

and then hand dipped in chocolate. She says customers come from miles around, year-round, for the signature sweet, a fan favorite especially popular for gifting. It's not unusual for Tickled Sweet's production area to fill up with boxes to be shipped, whether it be for individual holiday presents or corporate year-end appreciation gifts.

Six years in, Tickled Sweet has successfully grown into its space, garnering awards including *Cincinnati Magazine*'s Best of the North for Chocolates and Best of the East for Desserts, as well as Hula Frog's Most Loved Chocolate for several years. But it's Bambi's commitment to her community that makes her most proud of local designations such as SCORE Business of the Year and the City of Milford's Economic Development Award. A strong promoter of the area, Bambi welcomes visitors to historic Milford and its rapidly growing strip of retail shops, restaurants, antique stores and even a brewery and distillery, saying it's "a desired destination for evening events and exceptional dining." Community events such as Frontier Days in June, Sparks in the Park over the July Fourth weekend and Hometown Holidays over the Thanksgiving weekend bring people from all over the area to enjoy carolers, fire engine rides and holiday music.

Left, top: Tickled Sweet's signature buckeye candy. *Tickled Sweet.*

Left, bottom: Tickled Sweet's seasonal peppermint bark. *Tickled Sweet.*

Right: Tickled Sweet's white chocolate blueberry bar, featuring the shop's slogan, "Be Happy. Eat Chocolate." *Tickled Sweet.*

And those visitors come for candy, especially those who are in the know about Bambi's selection of cocoa bombs and peppermint bark, made annually in partnership with Doscher's Candy in Newtown, Ohio. "Doscher's is well known for their peppermint candy, and they provide Tickled Sweet with their peppermint chips that go into our dark and white chocolate peppermint bark and high-in-demand peppermint cocoa bombs," she says, adding that the relationship is reciprocal. "You can get our peppermint bark and cocoa bombs at Doscher's!"

Other partnerships include Sweet Hunter, a specialty dessert shop located in the Mount Lookout neighborhood of Cincinnati, which features delicious gelato alongside Tickled Sweet's artisanal chocolates, as well as Kala Coffeehouse in Mason, for which Bambi produces handmade espresso bars.

CANDY AS COMMUNITY

With a place in her heart for the underserved, Bambi hopes to help her community as it continues to grow alongside her business. In addition to Tickled Sweet's for-profit partnerships, she has two other sweet arrangements, both with local not-for-profits:

- Each fall, SonRise's Backpack Program supplies local schoolchildren with all of their back-to-school necessities, plus a sweet start from a selection of Tickled Sweet treats.
- After trick-or-treat, extra Halloween candy is collected and donated to Kingdom Warriors, a Milford-based group that feeds and clothes the homeless, hooked and hurting in the Greater Cincinnati area.

Believing in both her business and its historic hometown, Bambi believes Tickled Sweet will only continue to grow and prosper alongside the exceptional economic development of Milford. "One thing we know is that people like good chocolate," she remarks. "When they come into the shop, we often hear them jokingly say that they shouldn't buy much candy. And that's the point: it doesn't take a lot of good chocolate to be satisfied. We feel that good well-crafted chocolate will always be desired."

HAUTE CHOCOLATE

Lisa Cooper Holmes digs deep into the origins of chocolate when quoting what the Mayan culture is said to have thought of the idea of heaven: "To dwell beneath the benevolent shade of the Theobroma cacao tree, perpetually refreshed with chocolate." Thankfully for modern-day pleasure seekers, there's no need to travel back to ancient Mesoamerica, as Lisa has gathered the fruits of selected chocolate plantations and brought them to Montgomery, Ohio, to create what she deems "tempting, tasteful delights exclusively for your pleasure."

In business since 1983, Lisa's expression of this utopian dream, Haute Chocolate, started off as a challenge. A Cincinnati-area bakery offered her the opportunity to bake a better double chocolate chip fudge brownie, and

Cross-section of Anthony-Thomas buckeye and truffle candies. *Anthony-Thomas Candy Co.*

Teresa Jacques behind the counter at her pet-focused bakery, the Cakehound, where Bucks for Pups are a signature snack. *The Cakehound.*

This page: Danika Romick adds the finishing touches to a batch of her signature buckeye candies at the Buckeye Co. *The Buckeye Co.*

Creamy and delicious, milk chocolate peanut butter buckeye candies from Lancaster's Candy Cottage. *K Rodenbaugh*.

The Chocolate Café serves its namesake all day in dishes and desserts, including this showstopping buckeye cupcake. *The Chocolate Café.*

A box of Coblentz Chocolate Company's best-selling buckeye candy, hand dipped in the heart of Ohio's Amish country. *Coblentz Chocolate Company.*

Little buckeye candies atop Little Ladies Soft Serve's always delicious Aggie sundae. *Phil Navatsyk*.

Someone stole a slice of Aggie Pie, Little Ladies Soft Serve's homage to its home state's signature buckeye candy. *Phil Navatsyk*.

Train depot turned candy emporium Marie's Candies in West Liberty, Ohio. *Marie's Candies.*

A signature sampling of Marie's Candies beautiful buckeyes. *Marie's Candies.*

This page: Passing the torch between generations at Marie's Candies. *Marie's Candies*.

Left: A look inside a sampling of Honadle's Fine Chocolates favorite treats, including those named for family members, via cross-section. *Honadle's Fine Chocolates.*

Below: Two words: buckeye pizza. At the one and only Sweetie's Chocolates at Grandpa's Cheesebarn. *Sweetie's Chocolates.*

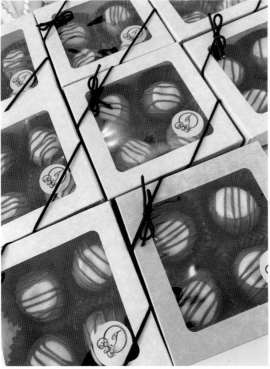

Above: A Blessing Box full of buckeyes from Tana's Tasty Treats. *Tana's Tasty Treats*.

Left: Perfectly packed and ready to pick up, Tana's Tasty Treats' signature drizzled buckeyes. *Tana's Tasty Treats*.

Left: Take your pick at Tickled Sweet from buckeyes made with milk or dark chocolate. *Tickled Sweet*.

Below: Counters full of chocolate cater to your sweet tooth at Tickled Sweet in historic downtown Milford. *Tickled Sweet*.

BUCKEYE

Above: A tray full of treats at Winans Chocolates + Coffees. *Winans Chocolates + Coffees.*

Left: Winston's tribute to Ohio's perfect pairing, the buckeye waffle upgrades its classic crown-style sweet waffle with complementary drizzles of Nutella and Reese's peanut butter sauce. *Winston's Coffee & Waffles.*

Buckeyes by the piece or the pound at Wittich's Fine Candies, Circleville's finest. *Wittich's Candy Shop.*

Perfectly packaged to please all palates, Wittich's assortment of white, milk and dark chocolate buckeye candies. *Wittich's Candy Shop.*

Debbie Smith and her dad, Jim Krenek, hand rolling peanut butter balls for the Goodie Shop's signature buckeye candy. *The Original Goodie Shop*.

Pretty painted artisan milk chocolate buckeye candies from modern maker Lohcally Artisan Chocolates. *Lohcally Artisan Chocolates*.

Top: "Go Bucks," a classic cheer for The Ohio State University, atop a classic combination, the Bellbrook Chocolate Shoppe buckeye candy. *Bellbrook Chocolate Shoppe*.

Bottom: A sampling of signatures including the Bellbrook pretzel, buckeyes and OSU-decorated shortbread cookie packaged pretty enough to gift (even to yourself) at Bellbrook Chocolate Shoppe. *Bellbrook Chocolate Shoppe*.

Above: Hand-strung designs indicate what's inside each Esther Price signature chocolate piece. *Kelly Schreck.*

Left: Hand rolling the three-times-bigger-sized peanut butter balls for Stella Leona Artisan Chocolate's "Not Your Grandmother's Buckeye." *Stella Leona Artisan Chocolates.*

Cut (or bite) into a creative twist on your traditional buckeye with selections such as turtle and sugar cookie Stuffed Buckeyes™ from The Buckeye Lady. *Devon Morgan.*

after she succeeded, they began carrying her product and also requested she develop additional chocolate products for their menu. Delivering on two extraordinary offerings, Lisa created her chocolate ganache truffles and peanut butter buckeyes. Popularity of her trio of treats grew quickly, and Lisa's family encouraged her to build on the business, making plans for a shop of her own.

After locating a historic property in downtown Montgomery, Lisa spent a year alongside her master carpenter father to restore and renovate, opening her brick-and-mortar chocolate boutique in 1988. Desiring not just a shop but an experience for her growing fan base, Lisa's marketing plan included a very liberal sampling policy. That policy now includes not only the original three products but a lineup of over three hundred chocolate and confectionary items created and produced in the boutique daily.

As a full line chocolate bakery, Lisa's kitchens keep busy with brownie offerings, including minis, heart shaped and even a brownie pizza topped with various candies per "slice." Seasonal specials include Lisa's Bunny Brownie Bundt, available around the Easter holiday in three sizes: trio, sextet and twelvetet. On the confections side of the house, signatures include

Haute Chocolate's milk chocolate buckeye candies. *Haute Chocolate.*

Buckeyes, Brownies and (Malt) Balls, Oh My!

A nostalgic favorite with origins dating back to 1936, the malted milk ball is a classic candy for many. Unlike the buckeye's creamy peanut butter center, this time-honored treat tends toward crunchy, though Haute's offering is crafted with a creamy chocolate coating. Flavor is where Lisa has fun, taking tradition up a notch with lemon meringue, raspberry and even mint Oreo cookie variations alongside classic milk and dark chocolate options. And because it's all about the namesake ingredient at Haute Chocolate, Lisa combines three types in her ultimate malt ball offering, which she says are "sure to become a staple in that candy bowl of yours or your private stash."

chocolate-covered Oreos and pretzels, as well as the "Great Pyramids of Lisa," described as "bite-sized jewels filled with our proprietary creamy, dreamy centers and lightly dusted with edible glitter to help with the discovery of flavor." In flavors ranging from milk strawberry to white Key lime, dark coconut and dark caramel toffee, it's a shareable taste trip for two packaged in a heart-shaped, ribbon-adorned box.

But it's the buckeyes that have never left the top three of bestsellers since their introduction in Lisa's original lineup. Since her first batch in 1979, she has lovingly crafted the creamy peanut butter center and catered to all chocolate preferences by offering them enrobed in classic milk chocolate as well as white and dark (an assortment of all three offers yet another signature tasting experience). Ranked among the top five in *USA Today*'s 2019 Reader's Choice 10Best, the golf ball–sized treats also appear in Haute Chocolate's holiday offerings such as the Buckeye Love, a heart-shaped collection that also includes heart-shaped foil-covered chocolates, and the Chocolate Buckeye "Treet," a similar offering in a Christmas tree–shaped box. At Easter, the box takes an egg shape for Haute's "Most Egg-cellent Buckeyes" or even more uniquely in the "Decadent Dozen," an assortment alongside caramel hunks, as well as chocolate caramel, pecan and malt ball chocolate geodes, in a thematically appropriate egg carton.

On brand with the shop's logo, which features a cartoon pig, Haute also offers a sampler referred to as the "Pignic" Basket, an homage to the city's moniker as "Porkopolis," which stems from its pork-producing heritage. Full of favorites, the package includes Lisa's mini nutless double chocolate chip fudge brownies, crunchy caramel corn, assorted chocolate-dipped pretzels, the shop's "Triple Threat" (a signature offering that combines one each of their buckeye, caramel hunk and pecan chocolate geode) and then another Haute hallmark, the white chocolate, creamy caramel-filled deviled egg. An exact replica of its savory sister offering, Haute's deviled egg is topped with a combination of marshmallow, rice "crispies" and white chocolate for a fantastic layer of flavor and mouthfeel and adorned with red sugar to resemble paprika. The incredibly creative, if perhaps initially a bit confusing, take on the classic picnic treat has become a year-round Haute fan favorite.

Those fans continue to inspire Lisa as they not only support but also help promote Haute's robust and ambitious offerings. Partnering with customers to plan celebrations from corporate events to weddings, Lisa loves designing and fulfilling confectionary visions. Nearing thirty-five years in business, Lisa is proud that Haute Chocolate is still residing, baking and creating with what she calls "chocolatitude" in Montgomery. A can't-miss stop on the Ohio Buckeye Candy Trail, she invites all chocophiles to partake in the joyful experience of sampling Haute Chocolate's creations with only a subtle warning, also the shop's tagline: "Our Strength…Your Weakness."

CHOCOLATE AND PEANUT BUTTER: A QUINTESSENTIAL COMBINATION; THE BUCKEYE: AN INEXTRICABLE INSPIRATION

Inextricably linked with the state of Ohio, the buckeye candy has inspired and is incorporated into a wide variety of signature dishes across the state—from pancakes to brownies, milkshakes to martinis, and dessert dips to not-so-classic cream puffs. Here are a few highlights from the heart of it all:

- **Buckeye Donuts, the Buckeye Donut**
  The Barouxis and Sauter families have kept this landmark, an Ohio State University campus institution since its opening in 1969, open 24/7, 365 days a year for three generations. Serving a full menu of diner-style Greek classics, including gyros, the shop has welcomed visitors from sports legends George Steinbrenner and Woody Hayes to musicians Prince, Foster the People and Akron's own the Black Keys.

The namesake offering, the buckeye donut, is a classic yeast donut covered in chocolate icing with a generous smear of peanut butter covering the typical hole in the center. It's even inspired a collaboration with local brewer Land Grant and coffee roaster Stauf's to create Open Always, a peanut butter coffee chocolate brown ale, which features the shop's logo, a cartoon chef Buckeye holding a donut. For those who prefer a nonalcoholic pairing, try the iced buckeye latte, the perfect double down with a buckeye donut.

- **Jeni's Splendid Ice Creams, the Buckeye State (aka Salted Peanut Butter with Chocolate Flecks)**
Though the latter name is its current iteration, early adopters to the Jeni's craze (which has since taken most, if not all, of the country by storm) still order this early classic by its original title, a true homage to the birthplace of the business. It's a twist on a typical chocolate and peanut butter pairing, flipping the script in preference of a peanut butter base (because, after all, it's the heart of the candy itself) made of grass-grazed milk combined with salted, roasted ground peanuts and speckled throughout with crunchy, rich, dark Belgian chocolate flecks.

  The company's website (which ships nationwide) description gives context to those unfamiliar, calling the creation a "loving tribute to Ohio and our signature candy," as it aptly describes its origins as follows: "In the Buckeye State (aka Ohio, where we are headquartered), one two-bite sweet is revered above all others: Buckeye candies. Designed to look like a nut from a buckeye tree, they are little rounds of creamy dark chocolate filled with rich peanut butter. And they are everywhere. Grocery stores to gas stations, gourmet chocolate shops to grandma's kitchen….It's total comfort for Buckeyes—and Buckeyes at heart."

- **Winston's Coffee & Waffles, Buckeye Waffle**
A newer addition to the well-established Columbus food truck scene, Winston's Coffee & Waffles is a product of the pandemic, as owner Steve Elshoff was poised to open a brick-and-mortar combo coffee shop and wine bar just as COVID-19 took hold in Ohio. With a pivot that also provided inspiration for the business's name (Sir Winston Churchill, whose attitude toward resilience in trying times seemed apropos for history buff Elshoff), Winston's set up shop in a semi-permanent location across from a popular local grocer in the Clintonville neighborhood.

Success followed in the form of fan favorite offerings including, of course, the buckeye, a sweet, Liege-style waffle (a style the shop's website says is "made heavenly thanks to caramelized pearl sugar" that is incorporated into the batter) topped with Reese's peanut butter sauce and not chocolate but Nutella. This dynamic duo is a fun departure yet close enough combination that indicates Elshoff's commitment to another saying of Churchill's: "My tastes are simple: I am easily satisfied with the best." The advice seems to be well taken, as Winston's opened a second outpost as a tenant of the East Market, a renovated trolley barn turned food court, which opened in April 2022 in the historic Franklin Park neighborhood.

- **Little Ladies Soft Serve, Aggie Sundae/Pie**
Another initially mobile operation that still runs its truck seasonally, Little Ladies Soft Serve likewise expanded into a brick-and-mortar location driven by the success of private events and neighborhood appearances during the pandemic. While Lydia Chambers's truck has been roaming the streets of Columbus (from Galena, its hometown, to downtown Columbus and everywhere in between) since 2018, the shop opened its doors in Westerville in the fall of 2021. The operation has also expanded to be a full family affair, with brother Phil Navatsyk and his wife, Kourtney, joining to manage truck engagements and social media and help run the shop.

Left: Little Ladies Soft Serve leverages itty-bitty buckeye candies in its biggest seller, the Aggie sundae. *Phil Navatsyk.*

Right: Buckeye pie? Say no more, and grab a spoon, at Little Ladies Soft Serve. *Phil Navatsyk.*

With a menu full of whimsical creations given vintage names (including three named after the owner's own little ladies, daughters Ida, Mabel and Flannery), the homage to the buckeye has been a staple since day one. The aptly named Aggie features a triple threat of toppings, all of which add both chocolate and peanut butter flavor and texture. First, there's crushed puppy chow, a midwestern sweet snack mix made of Chex cereal, melted chocolate, peanut butter and powdered sugar, which Lydia originally crafted in her home kitchen (among multiple mix-ins that are insanely delicious on their own). A double dose of sauces includes both hot fudge and peanut butter and then, of course, the crowning jewel, a smattering of buckeye candies.

The sundae is so popular that Little Ladies has joked on Instagram that it "pays the mortgage," and it was the winner in both 2021 and 2022 of the shop's March Madness Sundae Championship, a bracket-style competition. In 2021, it bested the Lucille, a seasonal special featuring pie crust crumble, blueberry compote and lemon curd, all adorned with a lemon cookie. In 2022, it beat out the Ruby, another fruit-focused sundae (candied pretzels, strawberry shortcake crumble, strawberry compote, whipped cream and a cherry). Per the shop's social media, it was a "clean sweep for the Aggie from start to finish, which makes everything in the world feel right." To cut down the nets on its win, the Aggie was offered at a discounted price on April 1, now known as "Aggie Day" at the shop after a 2021 April Fool's joke by a subset of the team caused an uproar after indicating its potential removal from the menu. Never fear, as leadership confirmed in a make-good post that "as a way to make things right and assure you that Aggie will never leave LLSS, we are declaring EVERY April 1st 'Aggie Day' (call off work if you see fit). *FOR THE RECORD, those responsible for the post are NOT sorry, and they still think it was hilarious. They also think 'Aggie Day' was invented to hamstring their future April Fool's plans.*"

Not only is the Aggie not going anywhere, but its popularity positioned it well to become one of the offerings among the shop's newest addition, the ice cream pie. Alongside menu mainstays including the Lola, Myra and Ruby, the Aggie has been translated to pie form perfect for celebrations (the shop also serves slices if you prefer to have a party of one). Place an order forty-eight hours prior to ensure you can snag this hefty helping of peanut butter soft serve, vanilla soft serve and chocolate whipped cream, layered with hot fudge, peanut butter sauce and puppy chow, all in an Oreo crust and topped with chocolate chips and signature flavor signal, mini buckeyes. Truly a treat for both the eyes and the taste buds alike.

- **La Dolce 'Nola, Buckeye Granola**
Named after the owners' two-year-old's preferred abbreviation, 'Nola, short for granola, brought together the Dolce family's heritage of food preparation. Inspired by influences ranging from the south of both the United States and Italy (Sicily to be exact), the family first tried their hand at making granola recipes with the intention of gifting them to family and friends during the 2020 holiday season.

Recipients clamored for more, and the company was born, with three signature flavors, spiced apple (features cranberries as well as homemade ginger cinnamon apple chips), midnight (a dark chocolate base with Start your morning off with a burst of buckeye granola goodness from La Dolce 'Nola. *Greg and Millie Dolce.* tropical notes of sweet hibiscus and dried coconut) and buckeye, a blend they refer to as the "classic combination from the heart of the Buckeye State." Featuring dark chocolate chunks, natural peanut butter and a custom blend of local favorite Krema Nut Company peanuts, fans say it's not overly sweet but well balanced and has versatility to enhance everything from your morning oatmeal or yogurt to a decadent dessert when swapped in for the streusel atop a fruit crumble or crisp.

- **Schmidt's Sausage Haus**
An institution in the Columbus neighborhood of German Village since its opening in 1967 (the family's meatpacking legacy dates back even further, to 1886), Schmidt's Sausage Haus has many fan favorite menu items, including the Bahama Mama sausage and its signature sweet, the Jumbo Cream Puff. Weighing in at a half pound, the oversized dessert is described on the restaurant's website as an "award-winning combination of special whipped filling in a lightly baked pastry shell." It's available in vanilla and a seasonally rotating flavor of the month,

but the buckeye-inspired chocolate and peanut butter fudge is a tribute worth tasting.

Right next to the restaurant is Schmidt's Fudge Haus, a stop on the Ohio Buckeye Trail, which uses an old-world chocolate-making process for its gourmet buckeyes. Make it a two-for-one trip to double down on deliciousness.

- **Krema Nut Company**
Another legendary Columbus company dating back to the nineteenth century, Krema Nut Company has served the community from its Grandview location since 1898. Still family owned, the business is one of the oldest peanut butter makers in the United States, focusing on small batches of hand-roasted nuts as well as a wide array of snacks and sweets. One of its bestsellers is the bespoke buckeye crunch, described as "America's favorite combination of peanut butter, chocolate and caramel corn." Touting its "handmade deliciousness," the product's packaging promises "one bite and this crunch will make you smile!"

- **Johnson's Real Ice Cream**
A Bexley landmark since 1950, Johnson's Real Ice Cream (with locations also in Dublin and New Albany) offers a few takes on the classic PB&C combo, including not one but two ice cream flavors: Buckeye Fever, a peanut butter ice cream with chocolate chips, and its opposite, PB Choco Tornado, featuring chocolate ice cream with a peanut butter swirl. Taking things even further, the shop also created a buckeye ice cream sandwich, peanut butter ice cream between two special recipe double chocolate chip cookies from Columbus bakery C. Krueger's.

A "cooler" take on the state's signature sweet: ice cream buckeyes from Johnson's Real Ice Cream. *Johnson's Real Ice Cream.*

But for the best bespoke bite and closest cousin to the beloved candy buckeye, fans go directly for the replica ice cream buckeyes, which upgrade the candy's peanut butter center to the same only made of Johnson's peanut butter ice cream, still dipped in chocolate. These tasty tricks are a tailgate favorite, offering the best of both worlds for fans of the team and treat. Better yet, all of Johnson's peanut butter offerings are made in partnership with Krema Nut Company's peanut butter for extra local love.

CHAPTER 3

MODERN MAKERS

O n first glance, the uninitiated might easily assume that a buckeye is a buckeye is a buckeye. While the combination of chocolate and peanut butter is a classic for a reason, any true Ohioan will tell you that they can tell a Buckeye (capital *B*, as essential as the trademarked "The" in front of "Ohio State University") from a buckeye. Perhaps it's the bespoke blend (be it of brands or house-made ingredients) that their favorite producer uses to create the creamy peanut butter center. Or a certain preference for chocolate, be it milk (classic), dark (distinguished) or even white (an unexpected delight).

For a certain subset of newer producers on the confectionary scene, taking a twist on the classic candy has become their calling card. New spins from flavor variations to bespoke presentations bring a more modern touch to tradition. From size to sprinkles to stuffed variations, these modern makers have made upgrades without sacrificing integrity, balancing the familiar with a bit of fancy. Some have even opened the world of buckeye candy enjoyment to new audiences, catering to everything from dietary preferences to those who want to spoil their four-legged friends (yep, bucks for pups!).

STELLA LEONA ARTISAN CHOCOLATES

Nancy Bontrager Yoder says she has had a taste for exceptional chocolate since childhood. Recalling the fine European chocolates her father would

Stella Leona Artisan Chocolate's former storefront in charming Pettisville, Ohio. *Stella Leona Artisan Chocolates.*

bring home from business travels abroad, she has distinct memories of beautifully wrapped, flavorfully rich, creamy smooth pieces unlike anything she had previously seen or tasted. She felt loved upon receiving them, and thus began a lifelong love affair that would eventually turn into a business idea with the mission "Love People. Give Chocolate."

Starting Stella Leona Artisan Chocolates from her home kitchen in 2007, Nancy began to create her own recipes for chocolate confections, to the delight of family and friends. Operating as a cottage food business for the first few years, she worked with an accomplished chocolatier to create a signature style, which blends "the complexities of fine ingredients and the artistry that distinguishes Stella Leona Artisan Chocolates from others." In the fall of 2009, she opened her retail storefront in the small town of Pettisville, which she says is a slightly "off the beaten path location," specifically selected for its proximity to her home but also because it gave her the "opportunity to serve local people and bring something joyful to town."

Just four months after opening the shop with the support of her husband, Greg, he passed away suddenly of a heart attack, leaving Nancy not only with a young business but also a family of five young children, two of whom are adopted from Guatemala. With the support of family, friends and her single employee, the business was able to find a way forward and continued to grow as Nancy raised her children. After fourteen years in business, serving the community with a commitment to hand-crafted quality, she decided to cease operations after the 2022 holiday season to focus on the next generation: her grandchildren. Now remarried, she and her husband combined have fourteen grandchildren (and counting!), making it the "magic number," in Nancy's mind. "The season for growing a business is ending for me, as the season of grandparenting a growing gaggle of kiddos ramps up," she said in her Instagram announcement, adding, "I founded this business out of a love for chocolate and the joy of creating something that brings people together.…Life is short, dear friends. Spend it doing what you love, with people you love."

Love is the theme that carries through Stella Leona's product line, with meticulous attention to every design and detail, from the holiday tradition of hand-painted high-gloss ornaments; to the birch cream caramel, a bespoke original flavored with Alaskan birch syrup; to the Heritage Collection, a line of chocolates created in tribute to the business's namesakes, Nancy's grandmother Leona and her sister Estella. Paying homage to these two inspirational women to whom Nancy credits her "love for life, family and baking," she hopes to "honor them with the commitment to quality and attention to detail that are essential ingredients in everything I create." She recalls fondly that both women were wonderful pie bakers, hence the collection being themed around old-fashioned pie centers, including blueberry cream, pecan, rhubarb cream and old-fashioned cream.

Other sure to be missed items include the best-selling peanut butter granola bar, drizzled with milk chocolate, and signature hot chocolate shavings, which served as the basis for hot chocolate drinks both made to order in the

Stella Leona's Heritage Collection, a line of chocolates created in tribute to the business's namesakes, owner Nancy Bontrager Yoder's grandmother Leona and her sister Estella. *Stella Leona Artisan Chocolates.*

shop as well as packaged to make your own at home. The tuxedo, a blend of one-quarter coffee with three-quarters hot chocolate, brought many friends of the shop back in with a craving for the combination of caffeine and chocolate. Some of Nancy's favorites both to create and consume include her butter toffee, one of the very first confections she perfected; the dark chocolate truffle (she prefers dark chocolate, saying "the nuances of flavor aren't disguised so much by lots of sugar"); and her granola bites, almond and milk chocolate centers with granola, pecans and cherries, enrobed in dark chocolate.

She also has a soft spot for the shop's homage to its home state, the buckeye truffle, which she describes as "incredibly creamy and flavorful without being overly sweet." Creamy natural peanut butter combines with milk chocolate for the truffle's center, giving it the taste of a peanut butter cup. Nancy then dips it into dark chocolate and decorates it with milk chocolate to look like a tiny little buckeye. On the not so dainty and delicate side, Nancy's twist on the more traditional buckeye candy takes things up a notch—or three. Three times the size of a normal buckeye candy, Nancy's "Not Your Grandmother's Buckeye" is a peanut butter, butter and powdered sugar–based recipe, like the classic, but she adds honey and cinnamon to make the flavor all her own. And of course, it's dipped in dark chocolate, her favorite.

From her specialized hand-painted collection to truffles and caramels, Nancy's upscale take on all things chocolate has brought pride not only to her

Left: A grandmother to fourteen herself, Nancy Bontrager Yoder's "Not Your Grandmother's Buckeye" is as oversized as her brood and stands out with special touches of cinnamon and honey. *Stella Leona Artisan Chocolates.*

Right: Jewel-like chocolates lovingly packed to gift another or indulge oneself. *Stella Leona Artisan Chocolates.*

STELLA LEONA + SPANGLER:
CREAM PEANUT CLUSTERS REBORN

After a chance meeting between Nancy and Dean L. Spangler, chairman of Bryan-based Spangler Candy Company (which also produces Dum Dums and A-Z Christmas Candy Canes), Stella Leona was invited to partner on the re-creation of the original Spangler cream peanut Clusters. It was one of the very first confections made by the company, introduced between 1912 and 1913 and among their most popular products for decades. But Spangler's focus shifted toward hard candy in the mid-1950s, and production of the originally hand-crafted Clusters became mass produced. In 2006, allergen concerns caused Cluster production to be outsourced to an Indiana-based company, but after five years, that partnership was deemed unsuccessful, and the Clusters went out of production in 2011.

Until 2013, when, after three tries, Nancy perfected the original recipe to the exacting taste memory of Mr. Spangler, who deemed them to taste just as they had in his childhood. Made by hand in small batches and with high-quality ingredients, the maple- or vanilla-flavored Clusters are double dipped in chocolate. Reborn mostly as a historic interest, the Clusters were made available only at Stella Leona and the Spangler Store & Museum. Deeming the experience one of the most significant events of the shop's legacy, Nancy says, "It has been an honor to work with them and bring back this nostalgic chocolate confection."

A highlight of Stella Leona's legacy, bringing back the Spangler peanut Cluster in maple and vanilla. *Stella Leona Artisan Chocolates.*

family but to their hometown of Pettisville, the small town that she remarks is "not a place one would expect an artisan chocolate shop." As she prepares to shutter Stella Leona, Nancy says she's proud of "simply surviving as a business for fourteen years and being able to serve the community," adding, "Chocolate is something that makes people happy. My goal has always been to make enjoying our chocolate confections an experience that creates warm memories and fosters the appreciation of relationships. It is satisfying not only to have developed relationships with so many people myself but to have played a small part in helping customers express their love and appreciation to important people in their lives." Delivering on her desire to "create something lovely and to serve the people around me," Stella Leona loyalists will not soon forget Nancy's directive to "Love People. Give Chocolate."

LOHCALLY

Denise Steele has been hiding chocolate since she was a child, but the vibrant colors of her hand-crafted confections from relative newcomer to the Central Ohio confection scene Lohcally are so eye-catching, even her siblings (who likewise secured their own personal stashes of holiday treats such as chocolate turtles, nut clusters or pretzels) would have little problem uncovering these artisan gems. Since 2019, a loyal fan base has certainly found Denise's signature solo and duo truffles, caramels and premium bark, whether at a pop-up event, local small business retail partner or, most recently, available to order online and ship.

Lohcally Artisan Chocolates is a childhood daydream come true for Denise, who grew up in the small Northeast Ohio town of Hartville, where her mother worked at Hartville Chocolate Factory. Denise recalls the shop as "central to the community," adding that it was a place "where it was a guarantee to run into neighbors and friends." Between her maternal influence and paternal Belgian genes, Denise developed a love for chocolate, deepened by the family's penchant for visiting what she describes as "off-the-beaten-path shops," often traveling out of their way to do so during family trips. "My family may have been a little chocolate-crazy looking back," she laughs, saying that these traditions led her toward today in that "early on, I had a dream that maybe I could own a chocolate business someday."

But the path was less than linear, with Denise first studying business and chemistry at Purdue University, noting that while this was quite an unusual

Lohcally's lovingly crafted and decorated buckeye truffle, a sensation for the eyes and the taste buds. *Lohcally.*

combination of majors at the time, it would turn out down the road to be "incredibly useful for chocolate tempering and business ownership." After college, she leaned toward the former major as a career path, attaining her CFA (chartered financial analyst) and spending just over a decade traveling across the country evaluating small companies' growth potential for investment purposes. This experience gave her insight into small business differentiation, a knowledge base that would certainly help her find her niche in the competitive confection category. During this time, Denise also became a mom to three children, raising them and volunteering at the family's church, where she helped to build and organize a volunteer group of over one hundred people, including training and motivating them toward a mission of educating the church's youth about their faith.

Denise believes that each of these experiences contributed to preparing her for the crossroads that she came to in 2019, when, with her children mostly grown, her husband, Robert, encouraged her to enroll in Ecole Chocolat's Professional Chocolatier program. Through the course, Denise became even more passionate about the potential of owning her own locally focused fine chocolate business, learning about the multifaceted industry from culture to history, science to art. "Through my education, I became more convinced that chocolate is a universally enjoyed indulgence through which people treat themselves and others," she says, adding that while her original intention was to produce chocolates similar to those she grew up with, the program gave her insight into consumer trends in chocolate, causing her to lean into the artisanal side of the business.

In putting together her business plan, Denise focused on her mission to "produce exceptionally flavored and beautiful chocolate confections made from all-natural ingredients, artisan crafted in and for the Central Ohio community." While there are many layers in the chocolate industry, from value to premium to specialty, the "fine chocolate" subset includes both craft-bean-to-bar chocolate makers, who purchase beans based on flavor profile and craft bespoke chocolate, as well as artisan chocolatiers, who purchase fine chocolate to create signature product designs. Focusing on freshness and high-quality ingredients, these confections have a shorter shelf life than those in other chocolate categories (typically up to three months) and utilize artistic elements as well as "by-hand" production methods. As such, Denise starts with premium sourced chocolate from the Fino de Aroma category, an International Cocoa Organization designation, signifying the top 8 percent of quality standard in world cacao production that is "recognizably distinctive in its flavor as well as traceably and sustainably sourced from premium cacao growing regions." With unique flavor offerings, crafted in small batches, Lohcally's products are true to the name, leveraging "locally grown and sourced ingredients whenever possible" to deliver a "fresh product that tastes noticeably different."

Beyond taste, craftmanship, another Lohcally core value, comes through in Denise's eye for artistry. All designs are hand painted with all-natural colored cocoa butter, with stunning swirls, exacting stripes and whimsical dots in colorways that often offer a signal to the flavors hidden inside. Aiming to give customers a "wow" factor in both flavor and appearance, Denise's creations tease the taste buds as soon as they meet the eyes. From the signature s'mores truffle, a duo (the designation given to larger creations with multiple layers of flavor) that she calls "a new twist on an old favorite," which features a milk chocolate shell filled with caramelized white chocolate ganache with marshmallow and graham cracker layers, to a seasonal special, the sugar cookie dough truffle, a holiday favorite enrobed in white chocolate and dotted with shades of green and red, each truffle gets a distinctive, identifying design.

From mint to coffee, to a collaboration with Columbus distillery Watershed for both a Bourbon Maple Solo and a Banana Walnut Nocino Duo, Denise's offerings range from classic to adventurous and adapt based on seasonal availability and customer demand. Case in point, while the lineup has long included two twists on peanut butter, both solos—a milk creamy peanut butter and a dark crunchy peanut butter—Lohcally was in business for three years before adding its own homage to the state's signature version of the combination, Denise's buckeye truffle. Having heard from customers that they desired a buckeye offering, Denise pursued continuing education with renowned chef and chocolatier Luis Amado to master a technique that allows her to cut out the tops of her original chocolate shells after they are released from their molds. Added just in time for Ohio State University's football season, this addition to the lineup was released as a sweet surprise in August 2022. Offered in both milk and white chocolate options, which are sold in four- and six-piece combinations, Denise even decorated these solos in a splash paint style of the school's color combination, choosing scarlet, white and metallic gray for the shells.

Building her business in just a few short years from her home kitchen to a shared commercial space with Just Pies in Westerville, Denise is now looking forward to opening a retail storefront for Lohcally in the Powell neighborhood of Columbus (where Annie's Wine Cottage has been a retail partner), as well as retaining the established retail relationships she has across town at small businesses including Grove Sheek Boutique (Grove City), Meza Wine Shop (Westerville) and Fresh Start Bakery & Café (Delaware). Bringing together her varied background and experiences to build a business based on community connections has given Denise strong footing to share her lifelong dream of owning a chocolate shop. In committing to produce "premium quality, exceptionally flavored and artistically designed, local crafted chocolate confections" for Central Ohio, her hope is that "Lohcally Artisan Chocolates can bring the Fine Chocolate Industry to Columbus by serving the finest chocolates, educating the public about the history, quality and sustainability of fine chocolate and bringing joy to our community."

THE BUCKEYE CO.

The Buckeye Co.'s website defines the buckeye as "[buck-i] noun: the solution to every problem and the answer to every question; the perfect gift and tasty treat for every occasion." And for the mother-and-daughter team behind this growing business, Sherrie Butler and Danika Romick, the sentiment couldn't ring truer.

It all started in 2018, when Sherrie and her husband, Brenden, opened Jack B's, a mom-and-pop takeout restaurant in honor of his late father. A huge fan of The Ohio State University, Jack passed down his love of all things Buckeye, including the candy. As a nod to this family affinity, the buckeye and its leaf were incorporated into the restaurant's logo, and one of the very first menu items was on the dessert side: signature buckeyes in two variations, traditional Butler buckeyes and cookie dough Butler buckeyes.

In part because of their bespoke buckeye creations, Jack B's business boomed (so much so that it required a move to a larger location), and Sherrie asked her daughter Danika to take over buckeye production in 2020. Taking over the reins on such a sacred tradition, Danika brought both her artistic flair and creativity in adding to the

Danika Romick outside Jack B's, the restaurant of her mother, Sherrie Butler, aka "MawMaw Buckeye Butler." *The Buckeye Co.*

lineup, saying, "The more I made buckeyes, week after week, I began to think about the growth and potential the buckeyes had to be the star of their own show and business!"

Which is exactly what they decided to do in the spring of 2022, branching off the business to officially create the Buckeye Co. No longer just a side gig, Danika now produces over twenty-five dozen buckeyes daily and is constantly working on new recipes. From her traditional buckeyes to buckeye balls and newly introduced "Bursting Buckeyes," she considers her offering distinct, as it goes beyond a "typical" buckeye.

Starting with their traditional buckeye, the Buckeye Co. elevates their standard selections by offering them in assorted packages of rich milk chocolate dip and white chocolate dip, each alternately drizzled in white or milk chocolate and topped with Danika's favorite finishing touch—a dash of coarse sea salt. Customizations such as colored drizzle, sprinkles and cups can also be ordered to coordinate with events ranging from weddings to graduation parties to bridal and baby showers. For the holidays, Danika not only creates beautifully themed boxes in the colors of the season but ups the ante even further with buckeye bombs, quarter-pound buckeyes decked out with "all the holiday glam!" In addition to seasonal offerings for Easter, Valentine's and St. Patrick's Day, the celebratory lineup includes a Birthday Bomb, Party Time Bomb, Unicorn Dreams Bomb, Dino-Bomb and, of course, The O-S-U Buckeye Bomb.

Further expanding her product offering, Danika also developed a line of buckeye balls, which are cake balls/pops dipped like a buckeye. The top two varieties are her cookies and cream buckeye, reminiscent of everyone's favorite sandwich cookie, and the brownie buckeye, which is Danika's personal favorite because they're her two favorite things and "you can't beat the rich, dark, smooth texture and taste—so good!" She adds, "It tastes just like a brownie but looks like a buckeye!"

Recipe experimentation also led to a recent creation, "Bursting Buckeyes," which Danika describes as traditional buckeyes bursting with sweet treats such as jam, cookie dough or candy. Included in the fall lineup are her take on the classic s'mores, featuring "traditional peanut butter buckeye dough stuffed with a marshmallow dipped in milk chocolate, drizzled in mallow-flavored chocolate and topped with tasty grahams," as well as the chocolate espresso: "chocolate cake dough infused with espresso, stuffed with a chocolate-covered espresso bean. Dipped in rich milk chocolate with

Danika Romick lovingly packaging her assortment of white and milk chocolate buckeye candies. *The Buckeye Co.*

a chocolate drizzle." Other fan favorites from the fall sampler include pumpkin pie, caramel apple and cinnamon roll buckeye balls and even an everything buckeye: "traditional peanut butter buckeye dough rolled in everything bagel seasoning, dipped and drizzled in cream cheese–flavored coating." It's a clash of two classics, the savory and the sweet— enough to entice the adventurous and confuse the curious. And it shows just how committed the Buckeye Co. is to "making ALL things buckeyes in whatever that word can possibly encompass!"

Even while enjoying equally fast growth as her mother and stepfather's business, Danika's transition to focusing on the Buckeye Co. full time was not without its challenges. In fact, just as she thought conditions surrounding the

The perfect mix in a pretty package from the Buckeye Co. *The Buckeye Co.*

global pandemic were improving, a large unexpected hurdle presented itself, which she refers to as "the great peanut butter shortage of '22." Existing supply chain issues combined with a recall of the Jif brand made peanut butter difficult to source, with those who typically bought Jif buying up other brands, including from the supplier used by the Buckeye Co. As Danika recalls, "The kind of peanut butter you use in making buckeyes is *crucial*, so you can't just get anything off the shelves," adding, "When the only item your business offers is [made of] mainly peanut butter, it proves to be quite the challenge!"

But she's certainly risen to the occasion, reimagining the famous dessert from her mom's restaurant to offer a signature product not only for Jack B's takeout but at other local retailers such as Brinkman's Country Corner, also in Findlay, and Hurdwell Market in Danika's hometown of Arlington. The Buckeye Co. also supplies Danika's creations to another local baker,

SHERRIE AKA "MAW MAW BUCKEYE" BUTLER

When Sherrie Butler thought about her hopes of someday becoming a grandma, she excitedly anticipated what her grandchildren would call her, aiming for a fun nickname like "GiGi." She now has three little loves, two girls and a boy, whom she's spoiled with buckeyes since they were little, always sending them home with buckeyes after a visit. The treats were greatly appreciated, so much so that as they began talking, she became referred to as "Maw Maw Buckeye," which she happily approved as "the BEST Grandma name EVER!"

the Baking Company, for their cakes and cupcakes as well as for a variety of local events.

The future of the Buckeye Co. continues to evolve alongside Danika's dreams for the business. In addition to experimenting with different flavors, sizes, toppings and so on for her offering, she is working toward meeting the customer desire to ship product by getting certified in a new commercial processing facility. "Every corner turned unveils new ideas and opportunities!" she says excitedly, adding, "We plan to focus on a 'by occasion' platform—Birthday? Send them bucks! Wedding? Send them bucks! Anniversary?! Send them ALL the bucks!" Also in the works is a standalone storefront taking over the former Jack B's location, offering all the different concoctions she's dreamed up, which she indicates is "just the beginning of what we see for the future of the Buckeye Co.!"

CHOCOLATE CAFÉ

Fifteen years, a recession-driven near bankruptcy, a global pandemic and a second location later, Lisa Boyle can certainly proclaim (as her website does) that "Life Happens. Chocolate Helps." Lisa and her husband, Phil Wolfe, co-owners of the Chocolate Café and Chocolate Café Express, both in Columbus neighborhoods, are no strangers to the ups and downs of running a small business.

The pair's first venture was a video store called Video Central, which they shuttered prior to opening their current business in anticipation of the changing video rental industry. That venture was in part influenced by their time in the television industry while living in South Bend, Indiana, during which the owner of the South Bend Chocolate Company appeared on their morning show as a guest. But it wasn't until years later, after they had moved to Columbus, that they ran into him at an event at which he asked if they'd be interested in owning a franchise of the company.

Jumping at the opportunity, they purchased the building on Northwest Boulevard, a busy stretch between Upper Arlington and Grandview, in 2006, eventually opening the doors to the first Chocolate Café in September 2007. Just as their new venture was getting off the ground, the 2008 recession swooped in, nearly forcing the business into bankruptcy. Working diligently to stay afloat, Lisa navigated financial options, including lines of credit that helped them to survive the challenging economic time. She had only a short reprieve before her youngest sister, Robyn, who had helped her grow the café since its opening, died tragically in 2016 in a car accident. Lisa recalls, "Robyn had helped me grow the café, she was vested in it and she was excellent at the job. It was absolutely gut wrenching." Just months later, Lisa also lost her father to a heart attack, meaning that within the span of two months, half of her family was gone. But Lisa soldiered on, overcoming grief to continue serving the community of loyalists she'd built, which eventually would help her weather yet another storm: the COVID-19 pandemic. Staying open the entire time, she says, "I think customers appreciated our consistency and commitment to them and our delivery and catering flourished because of it." She adds, "The fact that we are still open fifteen years later, and that we opened a second location during the pandemic, is pretty amazing when I think about it."

That second location, a carryout-only model on South High Street near German Village/Brewery District, was critical to post-pandemic growth, as catering and event orders ramped up in a big way. Learning from her previous experience as the video industry shifted to digital, Lisa's anticipation of the future of the restaurant business is "in catering, takeout and delivery. And the easier you can make it, the better." She adds, "The pandemic upended the models, and it's all new and different now." In working to not only stay viable but also grow, the Chocolate Café takes part in festivals and fundraisers, rebuilding its full calendar starting in the summer of 2022, which required the extra baking space provided by the German Village outpost. Weddings have also ramped back up, for which the Chocolate Café is a local go-to, especially for their brownie and dessert bar offerings. Being

LISA'S LOVES

While chocolate is clearly king, ahem, queen, for Lisa Boyle, the full menu at the original outpost, the Chocolate Café, serves not just your sweet tooth. Breakfast, lunch and dinner, as well as alcoholic beverages, make it a perfect spot for an all-in-one meal any time of day. With similar emphasis on high-quality ingredients and fresh, made-to-order menu items, the café accommodates all dietary restrictions from gluten free to sugar free, vegetarian and vegan. Lisa recommends a few favorites if you can pry yourself away from the namesake sweet:

- **Lunch Love:** triple grilled cheese on Italian panini bread with tomato basil soup
- **Craveable Cake:** lemon berry mascarpone (featured often among the seven to ten different daily cake flavors)
- **Classic Cookie:** sugar, a recipe handed down from Lisa's mother's parents' bakery in Alliance, Ohio
- **Drinkable Dessert:** chocolate cake martini (OK, that one's chocolate, oops!)

closer to downtown, the second location also allows them to better serve corporate carryout clients.

Whether you head to the café for a full meal experience or hit the Express for a quick bite, chocolate is still the star of the show. From fudge cake to chocolate chunk cookies (drizzled with extra chocolate), fondue and hot cocoa made with real chocolate, it's a chocoholic's paradise, a dessert lover's dream. A classic case of candy selections holds Lisa's favorite, the dark chocolate malted milk balls, alongside truffles, turtles, toffees, caramels and pretzels of all variations.

But it's the buckeyes that take the cake, quite literally, featured in forms including cakes and cupcakes as well as liquified into drinks including a buckeye hot cocoa, milkshake and even martini. The chocolate/peanut butter pairing also combines in pretzel sandwich form as well as traditional and not so traditional takes on the classic candy. Buckeye flavor variations including Oreo, cookie dough and Nutella as well as seasonal swaps such as pumpkin are fun and always super fresh, as all are hand rolled and dipped daily. With proximity to The Ohio State University's campus, buckeyes of all kinds are always a fan favorite. Customers have shipped Chocolate Café buckeyes all over the country, especially their Buckeye Fan Box, which features one dozen each of the traditional buckeyes, buckeye pretzels and assorted truffles. When ordering around the holidays, Chocolate Café also offers completely edible chocolate boxes—a treat to house your treats!

Still partners with the South Bend Chocolate Company, Lisa admires other chocolatiers, including local legend Anthony-Thomas, saying, "It is so difficult to stay relevant over a long period of time, and they've done it." Tapping into trends while staying true to one's roots certainly helps, such as it did in December 2020, when Lisa decided to offer the newly popular hot chocolate bombs and sold three thousand in just that month. While it pushed the staff to their limit, this production paved the way for growth to the second space, giving them more room to work.

Lisa credits the vibrant, very supportive Columbus community for the business's ongoing growth and expansion of their bakery business, saying, "This community loves small business! When the pandemic hit, we had people go out of their way to spend money at the café because they didn't want to see us close." And they certainly haven't, weathering yet another storm and coming out on top because chocolate is love, and love always wins.

TANA'S TASTY TREATS

For Tana Fischer, a buckeye isn't just a tasty treat but also a blessing—both for giving her the opportunity to share her creations with a loyal fan base and also for those dedicated customers to pass along the love via an occasional promotion she calls the "Blessing Box." Using social media to raffle off a gift box of signature treats, Tana has just one rule: the winner cannot keep the box for themselves but must give it away to someone else. She says the contest was created as a way to "help us think about someone out there that may need a pick-me-up, maybe a loved one that's down in the dumps, or maybe a complete stranger that you see working so hard." She adds, "It's just all about spreading joy. The real win is how you feel when you're giving the box away."

Tana's been spreading joy in buckeye form since setting up her home-based business in November 2018. But she's been making buckeyes since well before that, starting around age twenty-five and gaining a following

Tana's Tasty Treats signature party platter of bedazzled buckeye candies. *Tana's Tasty Treats.*

of family and friends who frequently requested she bring her specialty to football watch parties. Detecting a distinct difference in her offering, it was this group that encouraged her initially to start selling her buckeyes. "I remember the hesitation and fear of my very first Facebook post wondering if anyone would be interested in such a specific product alone," recalls Tana, saying, "Word spread quickly throughout our town and even surrounding counties, and soon production reached the thousands, especially around the holidays." In fact, that Christmas season she sold 4,500 buckeyes, with the help of her parents and an aunt, a supportive and productive team.

Her buckeyes are known among Coshocton locals as the "creamiest buckeye they've ever had" and "not too sweet," praise she's proud of and believes sets her product apart from others. Even those who critiqued the category of candy as all tasting the same were converted upon first taste as they melted into the velvety smooth mouthfeel and were mind blown at how diffcrent Tana's buckeyes truly tasted. "It took many tweaks to my recipe to perfect my buckeye," she says, adding, "It's a uniquely creamy center that isn't overly sweet with a genuinely good quality chocolate shell. It's the combination of the two that has made it such a hit." And her signature drizzle on top of each buckeye has helped customers quickly identify it as a "TTT buckeye."

A longtime baker, Tana's background goes back to childhood, when, after participating in 4-H and developing an interest in cake decorating, at age ten she became the youngest in a Wilton cake decorating class at the local Jo-Ann Fabrics. Fueled by her creativity and passion, she went on to win best of show ribbons at the Coshocton County Fair and decorated cakes as a side hobby while working as a registered nurse in a full-time administrator role. When she became a mom, now to three boys, life got even busier, and most of her decorating work was dedicated to her children's birthday cakes.

When her buckeye business took off, hard work and dedication were required to manage the workload. "Finding time and balancing my responsibilities has always been a challenge, but when you're passionate about something it all just kind of finds a way to fit together," she says, adding that spreading joy and bringing happiness is ultimately her highest reward. "One of the things I love most about my business is the joy that my customers tell me the buckeyes bring to their recipient. Moms telling me that their child only asked for my buckeyes for their birthday, patients treating their doctors and nurses, grandmas sending them to their grandchild in college or moms mailing them out to their soldiers far and wide. It's incredibly humbling really and what makes me want to continue." While Tana doesn't (yet) ship her treats, customers have both traveled with them and sent them coast to coast as well as overseas, with her farthest location on record being Wegeleben, Germany, to the home of a family's previous foreign exchange student.

TANA'S SAVORY SPICES

No, that's not a name change for the brand or another side business. Tana's other offerings are still tasty treats, just on the savory side. Initially created when her family's favorite seasoning blend could no longer be purchased, Tana took to re-creating a version herself, using top-tier ingredients. Another instant hit with fans, her savory spices include:

- **It's All Good**, a proprietary all-in-one seasoning, which was her first foray. It is a "season all" that can be used on everything from chicken to pork, veggies to eggs, steak to French fries to take things from bland to anything but.
- **Hot Stuff**, her follow-up line extension, shares the same spice base as It's All Good but with the addition of home-grown dehydrated ghost pepper for a more "extreme experience!"

As a lover of all things sweet, including, of course, her buckeyes, Tana says she'd be "lost without my It's All Good seasoning. As a busy mom, I need cooking a healthy meal to be easy. My seasonings are gaining popularity for their simplicity. Life is complicated; cooking shouldn't be. And I think people like how easy it is to use one bottle and elevate a routine dish into something spectacular."

Local retailers also took note of her popularity quickly, with one reaching out before the end of her first season asking to carry Tana's buckeyes in her shop. They've now been sold at seven local businesses, including Rust Décor, Coshocton Supply Co. and Auer ACE Hardware. "It's a uniquely proud experience to walk into a store and see your product sitting on a shelf," she says, "or be walking through the grocery store to be called out, 'Hey, you're the buckeye girl!'"

In addition to seasonally decorated buckeyes sprinkled to match holiday colors, Tana's product line expands occasionally on the sweet side to include themed sugar cookies and hot cocoa bombs. She's also done special offerings such as the "BIG" Buckeye, the equivalent of three of her original buckeyes in one milk chocolate shell, for holidays such as Christmas and Valentine's Day; the "Puckeye," a round peanut butter Rice Krispie treat topped with her buckeye chocolate (named because the shape resembles a hockey puck); and a dip served with graham crackers and pretzels called "Buckeye in a Bowl."

Already a local favorite, Tana's Tasty Treats gained even more popularity after becoming a huge hit at the first annual Coshocton Chocolate Walk in February 2022. Of her hometown, Tana exudes pride, inviting everyone to visit and see that "Coshocton County is nothing short of a gem." She adds that it's "known for Historic Roscoe Village, [where] one can stroll back into the 1800s canal era by visiting the unique shops and restaurants. There is no shortage of outdoor recreation between beautiful gardens, hunting, fishing, wineries, restaurants and shopping. You'll also love the small-town culture and friendly faces that make it such a special place."

And Tana's Tasty Treats are equally as special to the town that shares equal admiration for her talent. She's become known for her buckeyes as not just a holiday staple but a year-round treat, with fans ordering for special events as well as picking up a package "just because." Leaning into an unexpected business opportunity and overcoming what she recalls as "self-doubt and fear of the unknown," Tana says she's proud to have "learned that I really could be a female entrepreneur using my creativity to guide the direction of my very own business."

As for the future of her budding buckeye business? "I think we can count on the stability of sweet treats to stick around for centuries to come," Tana predicts, noting that the confectionary industry dates back to the 1800s. "As for Tana's Tasty Treats, I'm along for the ride and look forward to continuing to share my buckeyes and whatever new ideas that come along with them."

THE BUCKEYE LADY

Alicia Hindman, better known in Columbus as "The Buckeye Lady," credits her mom with the ingenious idea to put a fresh spin on—or rather *in*—her classic candy for a signature take that became an inspired business venture. "For years I've had a strong love and talent for whipping up and sharing buckeyes, a peanut butter and chocolate confection shaped to resemble the nut from Ohio's state tree," says Alicia, at the time a school counselor who had the idea to use her expertise over spring break in March 2020 to raise money for friends in the service industry struggling with closures due to COVID-19.

Wanting to add something special to ramp up interest, Alicia took her mom's suggestion to add M&Ms, and the state's first Stuffed Buckeye™ was born. Her first effort not only raised $1,000, which Alicia spread across fifteen friends in need of support, but also had people clamoring for more. Though she had only planned for her philanthropic pandemic project to be a one-time occurrence, Alicia found herself with a strong desire to continue helping others, as well as what she calls "a life preserver of my own" after the tragic loss of her brother Jeremy. Her two beloved rescue pups, Ruby and Ginger, brought some comfort, but Alicia still sought a meaningful outlet to channel her grief into something positive. Bringing together three of Jeremy's favorites—The Ohio State Buckeyes football team, Alicia's classic buckeye (which he always devoured in a single bite) and dogs, for which they shared a love—The Buckeye Lady business began in his honor and with a continued focus on charity, this time for canines.

Initially working out of her home, Alicia's operations quickly outgrew her kitchen, and she began searching for shared space. She stumbled upon a small women-owned breakfast restaurant in Grandview Heights called Basic Biscuits, Kindness and Coffee. Hitting it off with owner Rebekah Hatzifotinos, Alicia arranged to utilize the shop's kitchen in its off hours, producing buckeyes while growing her customer base, flavor catalogue and, eventually, a team of employees. She spent a year in the two-hundred-square-foot kitchen but was ready for a larger space and began looking around town until she found a spot in the heart of Clintonville. Serendipitously, the two-thousand-square-foot spot places her just feet from High Street, Columbus's main artery, with Worthington to the north and The Ohio State University a few miles south.

Two fast fan favorites, The Buckeye Lady's toffee and turtle Stuffed Buckeyes™. *Devon Morgan.*

But even once the space was secured, opening wasn't without challenges, as the surrounding neighborhood experienced a multiple-day power outage in June 2022, just days before The Buckeye Lady's grand opening. Alicia and her dedicated team continued rolling buckeyes in the dark, hooking up her parents' generator to ensure production wasn't pushed back enough to prevent opening. Happily, the power was restored in time and the shop's shelves were stocked, with Alicia's signature Stuffed Buckeyes™, including cookies and cream, a bestseller and one of the original varieties after M&Ms. Of this fan-favorite flavor, Alicia jokes, "I have many entrepreneur friends in the dessert industry, and each of them state that if you put Oreos in a dessert—ice cream, cheesecake, cake, cookies, whatever it may be—it will be the best seller!" She adds that it's "funny but true!"

Other signature selections range from puppy chow to red velvet, toffee to cold brew coffee. The latter also happens to be one of Alicia's favorites because of its contribution from another local woman-owned business, Bakes By Lo, which has a storefront in Hilliard's Center Street Market. Stuffed with both cold brew buttercream and double espresso cookies, it's a perfect pick-me-up complete with a touch of crunch. Another partnership Alicia is proud of is one with the Cheesecake Girl, located in nearby Dublin, Ohio, which provides the namesake ingredient for The Buckeye Lady's cheesecake Stuffed Buckeyes™. Of both relationships, Alicia says, "Incorporating other women-owned businesses helps facilitate community and support in an otherwise male-dominated food industry," adding, "You've gotta try both of these. You won't be disappointed!"

Disappointment is unlikely, as there should be something to satisfy every sweet tooth among the more than sixty varieties of Stuffed Buckeyes™ at Alicia's shop. The sky's the limit when stuffing buckeyes with previously unimaginable combinations of cake, cookies, caramel, nuts, pretzels and even a boozy bourbon offering. The shop also carries sprinkles in the colors of every Ohio professional sports team, from the Columbus Crew and Blue Jackets to Cleveland's Browns and Guardians and Cincinnati's Reds and Bengals and, of course, hometown college namesake The Ohio State University Buckeyes. Orders can be customized with any combination of these, as well as rainbow birthday sprinkles, and come in sizes ranging from the four-piece "Cup o Bucks" or Artisan Gift Box to traditional 2-, 6- or 12-packs all the way up to party platters ranging from 60 to 120 pieces. Another fun customization, The Buckeye Lady can conspire with parents-to-be, creating buckeyes stuffed with the color pink or blue for a sweet gender reveal.

Seasonal selections from The Buckeye Lady include peppermint, sugar cookie and gingerbread Stuffed Buckeyes™. *Devon Morgan.*

Seasonal creativity drives Alicia and her team to experiment even further, from fall's apple crisp and on-trend pumpkin spice to holiday-inspired eggnog, gingerbread, sugar cookie and candy cane buttercream (that's just to name a few of the varieties included on The Buckeye Lady's annually anticipated Advent calendar, with a flavor for each of the days leading up to Christmas), some of which they bring back mid-summer for the shop's celebration of Christmas in July. Perhaps one of the shop's wildest creations was the Thanksgiving lineup, complete with pecan pie and cranberry alongside a sweet take on a typically savory topping, Everything But the Bagel seasoning (if local ice cream legend Jeni's Splendid Ice Creams can make a sweet take on the now ubiquitous flavor, why can't a confection?). Of having fun with flavors, Alicia remarks, "I have really leaned into creating new varieties with each change of season and holiday! I want Columbus to be excited to see what we come up with next!"

Of course, The Buckeye Lady still offers a classic for the purists, as well as a vegan option, both of which are also gluten friendly. And they've partnered with the Cakehound, an all-natural bakery for dogs also from Columbus, to carry a pup-safe version as well. But the dedication to four-legged friends doesn't stop there, as Alicia donates a portion of the proceeds from each and every buckeye sold, whether human or canine, to support the work of area dog rescues and shelters. Among the long list of organizations helped by purchases from The Buckeye Lady are Canine Collective, Citizens for Humane Action, Columbus and Delaware Humane Societies, Franklin County Dog Shelter, PetPromise and Rescued Ohio. Local organizations not yet on the list are invited to "bark at" Alicia for future inclusion.

Sweet surprise is in store at The Buckeye Lady. *The Buckeye Lady.*

The Buckeye Lady's charitable creativity has garnered her a loyal fan base, including many who stop into the shop to buy buckeyes to share with out-of-towners. "We have introduced this often unfamiliar treat to people around the world, including New Zealand to England, California to Massachusetts and everywhere in between!" Adds Alicia, "We ship nationwide, and our buckeyes have traveled all over the country!" And when hosting guests in town, buckeyes make the perfect welcome gift, favor or even wedding dessert, for which The Buckeye Lady has a full-service event cart available to rent. The sweet little setup also makes an appearance at farmers' markets, setting up streetside on summer Saturdays in Dublin's Bridge Park.

Cultivating a love for baking from a very young age, Alicia credits her mom, grandmother, great-grandmother and her Easy Bake Oven as influential in her lifelong journey from casual hobby to culinary career. Of the serendipitous nature of her signature offering, she recalls, "Oddly enough, although growing up in Central Ohio, buckeye candies were not a staple in my childhood home. However, I looked forward to snacking on them at our

The Band Behind "The Buckeye Lady"

Just a few weeks after the shop's grand opening, Alicia released a social media video with an unexpected endorsement from well-known American rock band the Goo Goo Dolls featuring bassist/vocalist Robby Takac and guitarist/vocalist John Rzeznik (whose guitar case featuring her logo sticker teased the post the day before). In her post, she shares that the nickname "The Buckeye Lady" actually came from her connection to the band, with this excerpt:

I've been keeping the Goo Goo Dolls "plump and happy" since 2012! A part of our origin story that hasn't really been told publicly is the nickname "The Buckeye Lady" originated from filling the GGD tour buses with hundreds of buckeyes and introducing buckeyes to people from all over the world!! Marrying their veteran roadie of 20+ years has led to many close friendships, a support system during long tour cycles & of course the fun of sharing an Ohio tradition to people from all over world!

Their summer tour kicks off tonight & I wish them a safe, healthy, & happy summer tour across the USA! You bet I'll be taking them hundreds of buckeyes to their Ohio shows in August!!!

A week later, Alicia partnered with the band for a "Rockin' Giveaway," encouraging her fans to donate to their favorite animal rescue or shelter in exchange for an official Goo Goo Dolls guitar pick and coupon for two free buckeyes from the shop, as well as entry into a sweepstakes to win an autographed Goo Goo Dolls item. The winner was selected on August 3 during the band's show at the Rose Music Center in Huber Heights, Ohio, at which the staff of The Buckeye Lady was in attendance.

family friend's annual Ohio State Buckeyes versus TTUN [That Team Up North, also known as OSU rival the University of Michigan] watch party! To this day, I can visualize the buckeye candies sitting on a platter in the dining room at Becky's house; they were my favorite dessert!" Even though she didn't know then that her take on the treat would be a point of personal pride and a bustling business today, Alicia is proud of her uniquely delicious, eye-catching confections and says she envisions The Buckeye Lady growing to have several storefronts, bringing her original Stuffed Buckeye™ all across the state of Ohio.

THE CAKEHOUND

Have you ever met a paw'stry chef? If not, you and your pooch may be missing out. But Teresa Jacques of the Cakehound can remedy that situation with one of her doggy delights, animal-safe, edible cookies, cupcakes and other confections. At Teresa's gourmet German Village bakery and boutique, canines come first, with a focus on fresh-baked, all-natural, limited-ingredient treats.

Founded in October 2018, Cakehound was created in Teresa's basement kitchen, and items were originally sold via social media as well as at pop-ups and pet events throughout Columbus. But Teresa's love of baking, especially for pets, goes a bit further back, starting with a curiosity for creating as a child. Her first foray into developing recipes dedicated to dogs was during her time at former Short North shop Three Dog Bakery. In her eight years there (until the bakery's closing in January 2018), Teresa refined her baking skills and learned how to frost and decorate treats. She believed in the bakery's mission to offer dogs natural treats, saying, "People are used to the old dried-up treats sold at the counter at your corner pet store, which your dog likely doesn't enjoy." She adds, "Once their pups get a taste they always want more and will even start to recognize the packaging."

The central focus on giving pups the highest-quality treats means recipes are carefully crafted and colorings are derived naturally from carob, peanut, beet, spinach, turmeric and spirulina powders. Teresa says, "A lot of love goes into each bite, and we truly believe both you and your pup can tell the difference." She adds, "Each cake and cupcake is mixed, scooped, baked and decorated; each cookie is rolled out, baked and hand decorated. We definitely are a different breed of dog bakery in that each goodie is incredibly soft so even the near toothless can enjoy!"

For the first three years, Teresa juggled a full-time job in the restaurant industry with an equally full-time side gig at the Cakehound. But with the restaurant closures during the early 2020 COVID-19 pandemic, she found herself with time to prioritize the business, and customers staying at home

The Cakehound owner Teresa Jacques with one of her favorite four-legged customers. *The Cakehound.*

with their pups all day were happy for a way to treat them. Expanding her online offering, she was able to meet demand, though she had to renovate her home kitchen twice to keep up with the custom cake, pupcake and cookie orders available for porch pickup and limited shipping. As business continued to grow, she began exploring opportunities to expand her online offering to an in-person shop. She eventually secured a lease in German Village and renovated the one-thousand-square-foot space in time to open in early September 2021.

All treats are baked in house by Teresa and a small team of staff members, which includes her mom and mother-in-law, who help out when extra hands are needed in especially busy times. She's carried over some similar items from her time at the previous bakery but added a plethora of new creations, including favorites that change with the season. Pupcake variations include polar bears, bunny butts, peeps, lamb chops, rainbow pride, hambarkers, monsters, turkeys and turkey legs, the Grinch and Santa hats. And her creativity continues on the custom cake side of things, as Teresa says, "People ask for all sorts of different designs, such as selfie cakes of their dogs or a couple of times the human (haha!), cakes to resemble their dogs' favorite toy, food, cartoon characters, dinosaurs, squirrels—the list could go on and on. No idea is too wild; don't hesitate to ask!"

But we're here to talk buckeyes, right? And isn't chocolate toxic for dogs? Teresa couldn't leave pups without her home state's signature sweet, especially since she says peanut butter is most dogs' favorite flavor. So she set out to create a take on the treat that's safe—leaving out the sugar and replacing the chocolate with carob. Organic whole wheat flour, local raw honey, vegetable oils and peanut flour create the peanut butter ball, which, once dipped, looks incredibly similar to people buckeyes. So much so that Teresa has seen people try to trick other humans with them, saying, "Trust me, they figure it out when they get a mouth full of dry cookie and bitter carob." She adds that it's likely best that the "humans visually enjoy them while the pups scarf them up."

A best-selling item, pup-safe buckeyes make a great gift and are popular for out-of-town visitors as gifts or to bring back home. They can also be shipped and stay fresh for up to six weeks. As far as she knows, Teresa is the only bakery making dog-safe buckeyes, and her partnership with like-minded dog lover The Buckeye Lady means you can snag her treats at their location as well.

Other partnerships include two local spots in Grandview: Doggie Day Spa, which offers a selection of Cakehound cookies, perfect for after a bit of puppy pampering, and Fangs and Fur, which carries cookies, cupcakes and bone-shaped cakes with celebratory messages such as "Happy Birthday" or "Let's Pawty." Back at her shop, Teresa supports other small women-owned businesses and tries to keep products as local as possible. Featured on the shop's shelves are a variety of raw/dehydrated treats sourced locally, as well as handmade accessories such as collars, leashes, bow ties/collar flowers and bandanas from brands like Cheerful Hound, Contigo Dogs, Doggish, Girls Gone Raw, Crude Carnivore, Creative K LLC and Yappy Scrappy Pawty Hats. "We are in the business of keeping the humans happy while they treat their pups," says Teresa, with the goal of giving "people a central location to grab items from all of their favorite vendors and snag some tasty, pretty treats while they're at it. When shopping with us, you help support at least seven small women-owned businesses!"

Loyal Cakehound customer Bogart is a big fan of buckeyes (the dog-safe kind). *The Cakehound.*

> ## Favorite FAQ: Can Humans Eat These Too?
>
> Technically, yes. The Cakehound is licensed and registered with the Ohio Department of Agriculture, and its treats are human grade, baked with whole wheat or coconut flour, applesauce, egg, pumpkin, carrot, honey, vegetable-based fat, unsweetened coconut and all-natural powders (never any dyes). But since there's no sugar, Teresa says you likely won't love them as much as your dog does…

Teresa also believes in supporting the community that surrounds her, another lesson carried over from her time in the Short North. Bringing a background in hosting successful community events such as Three Dog Bakery's Annual Easter Begg Hunt, Cakehound now hosts a neighborhood-wide event for both Easter as well as Halloween. German Village's Howlin' Hound Trick or Treat parade invites both dogs and their owners to dress up, purchase a ticket and travel around participating businesses collecting treats. Other holiday specials include prepared pup meals such as turkey loaves at Thanksgiving, shepherd's pie at Christmas, Scotch eggs at Easter and turkey burgers for summer picnics.

No matter the season, The Cakehound keeps it fun, stocking the bakery cases with a variety of treats to bring joy to customers and their canine companions. "Hearing folks talk about how cute they are and knowing that the dog is going to be so excited and gobble it up is the best feeling," says Teresa, who is excited about the future, adding that she hopes to see Cakehound grow into "a bigger space eventually, or even a second location. I'd love to expand the bakery and offer parties, space for photo shoots, etc. I'm excited for more people to learn about us and give me the opportunity to practice some more fun custom cakes."

BIBLIOGRAPHY

Books

Price, Esther, and Linda Otto Lipsett. *Chocolate Covered Cherries*. N.p.:
    Halstead & Meadows Pub., 1991.

Articles

Abbott, Miriam Bowers. "Short Order: Winston's Coffee & Waffles."
    Columbus Underground, March 17, 2021. columbusunderground.com/
    short-order-winstons-coffee-waffles-ma1.
    ———. "Treat to Try: The Buckeye Lady." Columbus Underground, June
    29, 2022. columbusunderground.com/treat-to-try-the-buckeye-lady-ma1.
Abdurraqib, Hanif. "A Brief, Cheesy Interlude | Hanif Willis-Abdurraqib."
    The Baffler, June 29, 2017. thebaffler.com/latest/brief-cheesy-interlude-
    abdurraqib#footnote1.
All City Candy. "Harry London Candy & Harry London Buckeyes."
    allcitycandy.com/collections/harry-london-candy-and-harry-london-
    buckeyes.
All Things Christmas—Christmas.co.uk. "Christmas Food USA."
    November 23, 2021. www.christmas.co.uk/christmas-food-usa.
Archbold Buckeye. "Ribbon Cutting at Stella Leona—Archbold Buckeye."
    November 26, 2008. www.archboldbuckeye.com/articles/ribbon-
    cutting-at-stella-leona.

Barron, Jeff. "Candy Cottage Owner Turned Childhood Love into Business." *Lancaster Eagle-Gazette*, April 25, 2015. www.lancastereaglegazette.com/story/money/business/2015/04/15/candy-cottage-lancaster-ohio/25828331.

———. "Iconic Candy Store to Relocate This Summer." *Lancaster Eagle-Gazette*, April 12, 2015. www.lancastereaglegazette.com/story/news/local/2015/04/12/candy-cottage-moving/25673883/.

Bizjournals.com. "CEO of Iconic Dayton Sweets Maker Dies at 92." September 23, 2023. www.bizjournals.com/dayton/news/2020/09/23/ceo-of-iconic-dayton-sweets-maker-dies-at-92.html.

Bracken, Drew. "Tana Fischer Is Spreading Happiness One Buckeye at a Time." *Coshocton Tribune*, March 9, 2020. www.coshoctontribune.com/story/news/local/2020/03/09/tana-fischer-spreading-happiness-one-buckeye-time/4470083002.

Bravomiamivalley.com. "Ohio Buckeye Candy Trail Contest." bravomiamivalley.com/ohio-buckeye-candy-trail-contest-p1623-210.htm.

Buss, Ted. "The Day Chocolate and Peanut Butter Collided." Times Record News, March 22, 2019. www.timesrecordnews.com/story/opinion/2019/03/22/reeses-cup-origin-chocolate-and-peanut-butter-collided-candy/3245894002.

Cleveland. "Sweet Success: Fannie May Back after Bankruptcy." November 27, 2010. www.cleveland.com/business/2010/11/sweet_success_fannie_may_back.html.

Columbus Dispatch. "Former Tremont Goodie Shop to Reopen Oct. 26." October 19, 2009. www.dispatch.com/story/news/2009/10/19/former-tremont-goodie-shop-to/23989973007.

———. "State's Claim to Largest Ohio Buckeye Tree Falls." June 2, 2008. www.dispatch.com/story/news/2008/06/02/state-s-claim-to-largest/23571356007.

Columbus, O., O. Smythe and Adair Prs. "THE HARRISON 1888 Log Cabin Song Book of 1840. Revised for the Campaign of 1888, with Numerous New Songs to Patriotic Airs." electricscotland.com/history/america/logcabinsongbook.pdf.

Cook, Adam. "One Sweet Setup." Ohio's Amish Country. www.ohiosamishcountry.com/articles/one-sweet-setup.

———. "Smooth…" Ohio's Amish Country. www.ohiosamishcountry.com/articles/smooth.

Daily Advocate & Early Bird News. "Winans Chocolates + Coffees to Be Part of Ohio Buckeye Candy Trail." October 5, 2018. www.dailyadvocate.

com/2018/10/05/winans-chocolates-coffees-to-be-part-of-ohio-buckeye-candy-trail.

Daniels, Scott. "A Passion for Chocolate." Ohio's Amish Country. www.ohiosamishcountry.com/articles/a-passion-for-chocolate-1.

Davis, Kelsey. "Passion for Chocolate Led to Reopening of Honadle's Fine Chocolates in Hartville." *Canton Repository*, December 11, 2022. www.cantonrep.com/story/lifestyle/food/2022/12/11/passion-for-chocolate-led-to-reopening-of-honadles-fine-chocolates-hartville-stark-county/69653564007/?fbclid=IwAR2S6yBcjmT26J3z-KicjZI-vRnnTkYfv-ZE9HAzVgnj-8n05E_ZzlaW-LrM.

Dekker, Nick. "The Best Way to Celebrate the Buckeyes Is with Buckeye Donuts." Breakfast with Nick, August 29, 2022. breakfastwithnick.com/2022/08/29/buckeye-donuts-best-donuts-columbus.

Eaton, Dan. "Grandview-Area Bakery-Café Adding Second Location Near German Village." Bizjournals.com, June 4, 2021. www.bizjournals.com/columbus/news/2021/06/04/grandview-area-bakery-cafe-adding-second-location.html.

Ellis, Nate. "The Original Goodie Shop's Sweet Treats Remain Lure for Customers." *Columbus Dispatch*, October 29, 2021. www.dispatch.com/story/news/local/communities/upper-arlington/2021/10/29/upper-arlington-iconic-businesses-the-original-goodie-shop-bakes-sweet-treats-remain-a-customer-favo/8568019002.

Evans, Anne. "How Big Is the World's Largest Buckeye?" Columbus Underground, August 2, 2018. columbusunderground.com/how-big-is-the-worlds-largest-buckeye-ae1.

Fisher College of Business. "A Commencement Marked with Congratulatory Confections." July 20, 2020. fisher.osu.edu/news/a-commencement-marked-congratulatory-confections.

Fisher, Mark. "Meet the Founder of a Local Chocolate Shop That's Been in Business for 35 Years." Dayton, January 2, 2020. www.dayton.com/entertainment/personalities/meet-the-founder-local-chocolate-shop-that-been-business-for-years/NzY9G7VaTDY2eCs7FkspmN.

———. "New Esther Price 'Dayton Strong' Chocolate Bars Make Their Debut." Dayton, October 21, 2019. www.dayton.com/news/local/new-esther-price-dayton-strong-chocolate-bars-make-their-debut/BhkZ4GHiWMIDMcgnI5yycI.

Franks, Sarah. "JUST IN: Boston Stoker and Esther Price Team Up for Tasty Collaboration." Finance.yahoo.com, February 16, 2021. finance.yahoo.com/news/just-boston-stoker-esther-price-151400142.html.

Froman, Alan. "Grove City Town Center: Grove Sheek Boutique Offers Variety of Chic Items." *Columbus Dispatch*, May 26, 2021. www.dispatch.com/story/news/local/grove-city/2021/05/26/grove-city-town-center-grove-sheek-boutique-offers-variety-chic-items/7433937002.

Harvey, Kayla. "The Buckeye Lady Opens New Location in Clintonville." *WTTE*, June 24, 2022. myfox28columbus.com/good-day-columbus/the-buckeye-lady-opens-new-location-in-clintonville.

Holmes, Debbie. "Ohio State Graduate Remembers Naming Mascot Brutus Buckeye Who Turns 50." *WOSU News*, September 11, 2015. news.wosu.org/news/2015-09-11/ohio-state-graduate-remembers-naming-mascot-brutus-buckeye-who-turns-50.

Institute of Culinary Education. "Giving New Life to Vintage Chocolate Molds." ice.edu/blog/antique-chocolate-molds#:~:text=Today%2C%20chocolate%20is%20molded%20in.

Jalavadia, Shreya. "Into the World of Chocolates with the 58-Year-Old Winans Chocolates." India Food Network, July 6, 2019. www.indiafoodnetwork.in/food-stories/58-year-old-winans-chocolates/?infinitescroll=1.

Kuhlman, Marla K. "Columbus Classics: Anthony-Thomas Celebrates Platinum Jubilee with Sweet Deals." *Columbus Dispatch*, September 28, 2022. www.dispatch.com/story/news/local/communities/2022/09/28/columbus-based-anthony-thomas-candy-co-celebrates-70-years/69514763007.

Lucas, Guy. "The Origin of Buckeye Balls." Newsroom with a View, June 10, 2012. guylucas.com/2012/06/10/the-origin-of-buckeye-balls.

Lyons, Melisa. "5 Things to Love about the Epic Dayton Chocolate-Maker Esther Price." *Dayton Daily News*, March 9, 2019. www.daytondailynews.com/news/local/things-love-about-the-epic-dayton-chocolate-maker-esther-price/OUZqfYo8l1tPiPBM0uPR2M.

Martin, Chuck. "Nuts & Bolts about Buckeyes." Cincinnati.com, July 11, 2012. archive.ph/20120711144924/http://news.cincinnati.com/article/20051214/LIFE01/512140324/Nuts-bolts-about-buckeyes.

Moor, Ashley. "How to Score a Can (or Two) of Warped Wing Brewing Company's New 'Esther's Li'l Secret' Brew." Dayton, November 9, 2020. www.dayton.com/what-to-know/how-to-score-a-can-or-two-of-warped-wing-brewing-companys-new-esthers-lil-secret-brew/TDY4VIG5KVAQPBFBKMEO5PSJDE.

NBC4 WCMH-TV. "The Cakehound Now Open in German Village." October 1, 2021. www.nbc4i.com/news/columbus-business-first/the-cakehound-now-open-in-german-village.

Neman, Daniel. "Peanut Clusters Hand Crafted Again." The Blade, February 5, 2013. www.toledoblade.com/Food/2013/02/05/Once-famous-Cream-Peanut-Clusters-hand-crafted-again.html.

Norah, Jessica. "Top Things to Do in Amish Country Ohio: A Great Family Destination." Independent Travel Cats, October 4, 2015. independenttravelcats.com/amish-country-ohio-planning-family-getaway.

Ohio State Buckeyes. "Brutus Buckeye." June 17, 2007. ohiostatebuckeyes.com/brutus-buckeye-2.

———. "Brutus Buckeye." June 4, 2018. ohiostatebuckeyes.com/brutus-buckeye.

———. "Brutus Tryout Information." June 4, 2018. ohiostatebuckeyes.com/traditions/tryout-information.

———. "What Is a Buckeye?" June 1, 2018. ohiostatebuckeyes.com/what-is-a-buckeye.

Post, Susan. "First Look: Chocolate Café Express." Columbus Underground, September 16, 2021. columbusunderground.com/first-look-chocolate-cafe-express-sp1.

Poturalski, Hannah. "Mmmm, Chocolate: Behind the Scenes at Esther Price." Dayton, April 20, 2015. www.dayton.com/lifestyles/mmmm-chocolate-behind-the-scenes-esther-price/rAkjHSQY1S0T5EXUShtZWP.

Powell, Lisa. "Esther Price, Dayton's Candy Company Founder: 'I Was Thrilled Every Time I Stirred a Pan of Candy.'" Dayton, October 28, 2021. www.dayton.com/news/special-reports/esther-price-dayton-candy-company-founder-was-thrilled-every-time-stirred-pan-candy/FXhH4ucImhedYES2QXLTQL.

Prinz, D. "Bringing Buckeye Candy to Experts." On the Chocolate Trail, July 20, 2015. onthechocolatetrail.org/2015/07/bringing-buckeye-candy-to-experts.

Pritchard, Edd. "Reviving Honadle's Candy: Family Brings Chocolate Company Back to Life." Canton Repository. www.cantonrep.com/story/business/2014/08/10/reviving-honadle-s-candy-family/36705739007.

Seman, Gary, Jr. "People Are Going Nuts over New Stuffed Buckeyes at Clintonville Shop." Columbus Dispatch, July 6, 2022. www.dispatch.com/story/news/local/communities/clintonville/2022/07/06/people-going-nuts-over-new-stuffed-buckeyes-clintonville-shop/7815852001.

10Best. "Best Buckeyes in Ohio Winners (2019) | USA TODAY 10Best." www.10best.com/awards/travel/best-buckeyes-in-ohio.

Trademarklicensing.osu.edu. "Traditions: Trademark and Licensing Services." trademarklicensing.osu.edu/page/traditions.

Valentini, Kyle. "Experiencing Chocolate." Ohio's Amish Country. www. ohiosamishcountry.com/articles/experiencing-chocolate.

Wiley, Chelsea. "Three Dog Bakery's Closure Sends a Clear Message to Small Businesses in the Short North: It's Only a Matter of Time." *Columbus Navigator,* January 5, 2018. www.columbusnavigator.com/short-north-high-rents-three-dog-bakery.

Wilkinson, Howard. "What Happens When Your Friend's Grandma Is Esther Price? You Get a Stomachache." WVXU, February 12, 2022. www.wvxu.org/food/2022-02-12/was-esther-price-real-person.

WLWT. "Esther Price Now Selling Dayton Strong Candy Bars." October 30, 2019. www.wlwt.com/article/esther-price-now-selling-dayton-strong-candy-bars/29634928.

———. "The World's Largest Buckeye Weighs in at 338.8 Pounds." August 3, 2018. www.wlwt.com/article/the-worlds-largest-buckeye-weighs-in-at-3388-pounds/22629491.

Wockenfuss Candies. "The Origins of Malted Milk Balls." March 14, 2022. wockenfusscandies.com/blog/origins-of-malted-milk-balls/.

ABOUT THE AUTHOR

A Buckeye not by birth but by choice, Renee Casteel Cook is a Columbus-based author of culinary history and travel titles including *The Columbus Food Truck Cookbook* and *Ohio Ice Cream: A Scoop of History*. Her passion for both writing and chocolate are equally matched, making this book a labor of nothing but love. Eternally impressed at the drive and dedication of food-focused entrepreneurs and the continuing commitment of generational family-run businesses, Renee strives to successfully share their stories, capturing a curated selection of legacies both established and developing. Her hope is to inspire future creators of all types to take the leap toward what they love.